"The many followers of Nopalito will be overjoyed to have this comprehensive cookbook that chronicles their story through classic Mexican recipes, gorgeous photographs, and practical step-by-step instructions. May this work inspire you and bring you closer to some of the most delicious flavors out there. Salud!"

—GABRIELA CÁMARA, RESTAURATEUR AND CHEF OF CONTRAMAR AND CALA

"What a thoughtful, inviting book! Page after page of beautiful, soul-satisfying dishes propelled me toward the kitchen to bring alive these honest flavors. These recipes were born from the real food of Mexico, then coaxed into a San Francisco existence at Nopalito under the guiding hand of Gonzalo Guzmán. As you read through the jam-packed salsas chapter, you'll find your heart beating faster and faster: so many flavors and textures, so much joy to be had!"

—RICK BAYLESS, CHEF-OWNER OF CHICAGO'S FRONTERA GRILL, TOPOLOBAMPO, AND LEÑA BRAVA, AND HOST OF PUBLIC TELEVISION'S *MEXICO: ONE PLATE AT A TIME*

"More than just a snapshot of a restaurant, *Nopalito* is an inspiring, enticing portrait of a cuisine. I want to eat this whole book. And with Guzmán's pantry-stocking tips, stories, and hands-on guidance, I'm ready to start making masa and working my way up to *platillos fuertes* (big plates) projects."

—ADAM SACHS, EDITOR IN CHIEF OF *SAVEUR* MAGAZINE

Nopalito

A MEXICAN KITCHEN

**Gonzalo González Guzmán
with Stacy Adimando**

**PHOTOGRAPHY BY
EVA KOLENKO**

TEN SPEED PRESS
California | New York

To the staff of Nopalito, past and present,
who have made this possible.

contents

Background and Basics: From Mexico to Your Kitchen

Platillos Pequeños (Small Plates)

Tacos de Cochinita 91
Marinated Shredded Pork Tacos

Tacos de Pescado al Pastor 95
Fish Tacos Marinated in Adobo

Tamales de Amarillo con Camote 96
Sweet Potato Tamales with Mole Amarillo

Tamales de Birria con Pollo 103
Tamales with Stewed Chicken

Tamales Empipianados 106
Tamales with Red Spiced Sunflower Seed Mole

Empanadas de Deshebrada de Res 108
Fried Beef Empanadas

Empanadas de Camarón 110
Fried White Shrimp Empanadas

Empanadas de Flor de Calabaza 111
Fried Empanadas with Squash Blossoms

Gorditas de Papas con Chorizo 113
Potato Gorditas with Chorizo

Huaraches de Huitlacoche y Hongos 114
Blue Corn Huaraches with "Corn Truffle" and Mushrooms

Tostadas de Picadillo 117
Ground Beef Tostadas

Tostadas de Tinga Poblana 118
Chicken Tinga Tostadas

Panuchos de Pollo 121
Black Bean–Stuffed Tortillas with Shredded Chicken

Arroz Mexicano 122
Mexican Rice

Frijoles Pinquitos de la Olla 125
Braised Pinquito Beans

Frijoles Pinquitos Refritos 126
Refried Pinquito Beans

Frijoles Negros de la Olla 126
Braised Black Beans

Frijoles Negros Refritos 127
Refried Black Beans

Vegetales con Aceite de Chile Cascabel 128
Roasted Vegetables in Cascabel Chile Oil

Platillos Fuertes
(Big Plates)

Chilaquiles Rojos con Huevos 135
Red Chilaquiles with Scrambled Eggs

Huevos de Caja 136

Frijoles Puercos con Huevos 139
Pork-Braised Butter Beans with Scrambled Eggs

Machaca de Camarón con Huevos 140
Smashed Shrimp with Eggs and Salsa

Guisado de Res de Pasilla 141
Stewed Beef with Pasilla Chiles

Caldo Tlalpeño con Pollo 143
Clear Chicken and Vegetable Soup from Tlalpeño

Pozole Rojo 144
Red Pork Soup with Hominy

Sopa de Pollo con Fideos 147
Chicken Soup with Fried Noodles

Tesmole de Mariscos 148
Spicy Seafood Soup

Birria al Res 151
Short Rib Stew

Bisteces à la Mexicana 153
Mexican-Style Stewed Steak

Carne Asada con Chorizo 155
Grilled Steak with Chorizo

Carnitas 156

Trucha Adobada en Hoja de Plátano 159
Adobo-Rubbed Trout in Banana Leaves

Tortas Pambazos 160
Salsa-Dipped, Griddled Chorizo and Potato Sandwiches

Tortas de Chilorio 163
Adobo-Braised Pork Sandwiches

Gemita Poblana de Milanesa 164
Breaded Chicken Sandwiches with Sesame Rolls

Enchiladas Rojas de Camarón 167
Red Shrimp Enchiladas

Enchiladas de Mole Poblano 170
Chicken Enchiladas with Mole Poblano

PREFACE:
THE GONZALO EFFECT

Maybe this is your dream, or maybe it's your nightmare: A chef leads you back into his restaurant kitchen, his sacred, private labyrinth, where, within an instant, cooks begin buzzing around you, clogs squeaking, triceps bulging out from either side of their bodies while they carry cauldrons full of sauce or balance broad metal sheet pans. You know instinctively you need to fall in line with the kitchen rhythm, not in a minute but right now, because as chefs slip and slink behind and around you, their intensity radiates it loud and clear: *Lady, you make one dumb move right now, and you will be wearing this mole.*

For too long we have been fed the intimidating notion that the professional chef's world is distinct and distant from our own. Restaurant food, we've been led to believe, requires a knowledge and artistry far beyond what we can achieve in our home kitchens. So we grow to believe we can't possibly produce those dishes ourselves unless we are wielding hypersharpened knives, heatproof fingertips, and white chef coats. Until we know how to masterfully coax a fresh farm egg into a cloudlike omelet or know by aroma the precise moment when a chicken is done roasting, we are left to assume we are best off cooking our fast-easy-fresh recipes at home and yielding to the pros when we want to be in awe of something impressive on our plates.

This, I've noticed, proves especially true with ethnic cuisines. Cooking international cuisine at home still carries an aura of difficulty. There is a lingering myth that foreign food demands more from us as cooks—more from our kitchens, our supplies, our spice cabinets, our schedules—than does continuing to make the foods that are already in our comfort zones.

This can all be very convincing, which may be one reason why the only Mexican foods most of us have attempted to cook at home are tacos and quesadillas. It is also why I am so honored and excited to help give the world a window into Gonzalo Guzmán—a chef with so much nostalgia, passion, and love for cooking the food from his Mexican upbringing that he wants to break down whatever walls it takes for you to embrace this cooking, too.

We're not here to tell you how easy it is to cook authentic Mexican food. Gonzalo, my coauthor and the chef of Nopalito restaurants, will be the first to admit that some of the recipes require a labor of love. But I have learned something essential from timidly following him around his San Francisco kitchens, my heart secretly racing with every pot lid that he lifts: although some recipes are admittedly longer, more laborious, and more capable of feeding a small army than others, the most difficult part about making them—or any Mexican food—is getting over the mental hump it takes to try. Some of the raw ingredients and techniques in this book may be (exhilaratingly) exotic to you, but chances are you will find the kitchen rhythms they require familiar—the whir of the blender, drum beat of knife on cutting board, and sizzling of sauté pans. But when the kitchen symphony dies down and the dinner bell rings, you will have something comforting, nourishing, *and* transporting on your plate.

My path to cooking Gonzalo's food was hardly seamless. It was only after meeting with him week after week and letting myself trust-fall into a world where I awkwardly botched the rolled *r* in every recipe title, Jackson Pollocked my entire kitchen trying to "fry a salsa," and risked squashing a finger every time I clamped down on my borrowed tortilla press, that I dared to say I was beginning to hold my own in my pursuit of Mexican home cooking. My homemade tortillas may not come out as geometrically perfect circles yet, but the recipes and guidance in this book have enabled me to stand in a Mexican kitchen or grocery and feel empowered and connected as a cook and human. Never intimidated. Never silly for having shown up to try.

Gonzalo is a tremendous, patient, and dedicated teacher—though I know he will be embarrassed by my saying so, even more so by my writing this preface. But I could not pass up the opportunity to honor his rare qualities as a chef and a person. Because once you know Gonzalo, you just want to do right by him. The knowledge and encouragement he has shared have led me to so many small but addictive triumphs, like choosing the perfect edible cactus paddle (look for bright colors and a firm feel), telling when a tamale is done steaming (a toothpick inserted into the masa should come out clean, but first, don't forget to open up the corn husk), and creating impossibly tender carnitas (it's all about the lard). But beyond imparting new kitchen skills, Gonzalo and this book project have helped me see Mexican culture in America in a way I hadn't before. How many times had I passed the Mexican markets in San Francisco's Mission District with little to no thought about stopping in? Now, I have a sense of quiet satisfaction bringing my guajillo chiles, epazote, and piloncillo up to the counter, and watching the clerk smile a little, wondering what this little gringa is going to do with all her Mexican goodies.

The ability to bring it all full circle is Gonzalo's greatest strength. He has found a way to honor his roots, the inspiration to infuse them with his professional culinary learnings, and the courage to open two restaurants about old school–meets–organic Mexican cooking in one of the world's most discerning food cities. Although reading how this boy from rural Mexico became a beloved Mexican American chef may make you wistful for your own romantic life story, the envy melts away once you realize that what has inspired him is pure nostalgia, hard work, and love for his family—not pride or a desire for fame. And, of course, once you own this book, you are privy to (almost) all of his secrets anyway.

Since I began working on this book, I have not stopped talking about this chef and his incredibly fresh, one-of-a-kind, Mexican-by-way-of-California food: to friends, to family, and (seriously? I'm sorry, everyone) to strangers. I keep doing this because the message is unfailingly well received. People love the Nopalito restaurants.

Some come from far and wide to visit them. Others come loyally and religiously with their families, week after week. But all of them see something special in this place and its message and are glad to support it. And the whole story of a young, successful Mexican chef cooking the foods his mama taught him is equal parts inspiring and heartbreaking. Hearing about Mexican cuisine from someone who loves it *so* much makes you almost homesick for a place you may have never even been to. You immediately want to take part in this world of re-creating humble—and humblingly beautiful—dishes, which, after seventeen years and counting away from Mexico, are still among Gonzalo's fondest memories.

Gracias, Gonzalo, for opening up not only your world but also the world of Mexican cooking, to me and to these lucky readers.

Estoy muy contenta que puedo llamarte mi amigo.

—Stacy Adimando

INTRODUCTIONS

I grew up in the tiny village of Catemaco in Veracruz, Mexico. From the outside, we would have appeared to have very little. My family tended cornfields, and my mom and aunt cooked for many of our community's town and school events, making everything by wood fire and without a refrigerator or even electricity. Looking back, I can see that those days of farming by morning and cooking family dinners from scratch at night—even without modern conveniences—made for a rich and memorable life. Of course, my life today as a partner and chef of two Nopalito restaurants in San Francisco is not so bad either. But in some ways, what I do in my kitchens here is an attempt to remember and honor the way things were back then—the food our days revolved around, and the simple life we led and loved.

With the time pressures of cooking, maintaining the restaurants, and raising my own family here in California, somehow the years have flown by without my returning much to Mexico, and when I have time and space to think about it, I deeply miss the feeling of walking the rows of our local farms, grinding corn every day on our communal *molino*, or relaxing in the shade beneath my late grandfather's cacao trees. I know it can never again be the same as it was then—I'm sure time has brought

changes to the village, and to my family's way of living. But there is plenty about the traditional experience we had that is worth preserving and sharing, even in the fast-paced urban lives many of us have. This is the inspiration behind my restaurants, and the pages of this book.

At Nopalito we do home-style, authentic Mexican food with seasonal, organic ingredients, giving the dishes fresh and delicious twists in line with today's ever-evolving food world. So as much as this is a book about Mexican home cooking—inspired by the days I spent accidentally learning it in my hometown in Veracruz and later in Puebla—it also incorporates the knowledge I've gained from the last seventeen years working in San Francisco restaurants, where I've had access to not only incredible local ingredients but also some of the best chef mentors imaginable. I hope you will use these recipes as a stepping stone to explore and experiment with Mexican cooking. Once you understand the basic ingredients and techniques of the cuisine—and hear the stories of the cooks, *mamás*, and *abuelitas* of our hometowns, who infused them with love, flavor, and brilliant color from their modest kitchens—the recipes and techniques will more easily become a part of your own home kitchen.

I had a hard time believing my co-chefs, partners, and chef mentors when they told me people would want to come to a restaurant that served the foods from my small-town upbringing in Mexico. To me, the dishes we ate were so humble, so second-nature, that I doubted that people in San Francisco, one of the best food cities in the world, would find them as compelling as I did growing up. I guess my partners were right—and the opportunity to cook these recipes every day and record them in this book is a gift I feel so lucky to have. This book is by no means the be-all, end-all guide to every dish in Mexico. It is a collection of the ones that have made the deepest impressions on my heart and live on in my memory most intensely since being away from home. Thank you for celebrating them with me.

—*Gonzalo Guzmán*

Unlike my co-chef Gonzalo, I really didn't know much about the food south of our border before we opened Nopalito together with our partners in 2009. I am a cook, a classically trained cook, versed in French, Italian, Greek, and Spanish cooking styles, but as of eight years ago Mexican food to me still just meant huge platters of beans, rice, and tortillas smothered with tons of melted cheese; burritos bigger than my head; and taco salads in their deep-fried, often stale shells. It was about sombrero-wearing waiters and strolling mariachi bands (why, by the way, does the shortest musician always seem to carry the biggest guitar and vice versa?).

Much of the Mexican dining scene in the United States is loaded with stereotypes and Western bastardizations. But I have been lucky to have small insights into the traditional culture and food by way of my Mexican colleagues, hard at work in every restaurant kitchen I've worked in over the last thirty-plus years. In my experience, these were almost always young men who had made the often dangerous journey from their pueblos to the "land of gold." Not many spoke English at all, forcing me to patch together my still embarrassing version of kitchen Spanish. Most had two jobs; were working sixteen hours a day, and were sending almost every penny back to their families in Mexico. They may have gone for years without seeing their wives, parents, siblings, or children. The daily stresses of being illegal or invisible in our society would have destroyed me. But to so many of them, it was motivation to work impossibly hard and persevere.

Not many of the Mexican cooks I've encountered in San Francisco have had a dream to become cooks. Many have come from backgrounds as diverse as teacher, lawyer, rancher, farmer, police officer, and government official. Cooking was and still is a way to get a job quickly, without necessarily having a lot of experience, and most have not ended up falling deeply in love with cooking. I have encountered only a few notable exceptions—in particular, a young man from Veracruz who stood head and shoulders above the rest.

Gonzalo González Guzmán showed up in a fancy Greek restaurant where I was managing the kitchen eighteen years ago. His father, Santiago, who was a dishwasher at the time, asked me if his sixteen-year-old son could have a job with us. I consented, and a day later a small, sweet, very young-looking kid showed up to work. I asked his papa if this boy was really sixteen. *Sí, sí,* he assured me. And that's when Gonzalo (who was really fourteen) and I began our professional relationship.

A few weeks later, a prep position opened up in the kitchen. To me, Gonzo—with his burning intelligence, speed, and self-motivation—was the obvious choice for the job. He excelled immediately and was soon a valuable member of the kitchen staff.

A little more than a year later, I left to open my first restaurant, a miniscule space in the Fillmore District that featured Mediterranean small plates. Gonzalo came along and began his career as a line cook. He remained there for several years, cooking in other restaurants as a second job, and thriving as both a cook and a natural leader.

In 2006, my partners, Jeff Hanak and Allyson Jossel, and I opened Nopa, a California-style restaurant with a wood-fired oven. Gonzalo had just become a father, and for a short time he had transitioned out of the kitchen to make some "real money" bussing tables at night in a high-end restaurant. He was my first choice as butcher for our new place, and after a lot of convincing on my part, he joined our kitchen at Nopa, once again quickly moving up through the ranks and becoming a sous chef.

Fast-forward three years: I was working one evening and talking with a guest about edible plants, including cactus leaves, or *nopales*. He mentioned his purchase that afternoon of a small nopale, or *nopalito*, and upon hearing the word I immediately had a flash that this was the perfect concept on which to build our next project. The very next day, my partner Jeff was approached to see a raw space less than two blocks away from Nopa. Aha! The concept of our Mexican restaurant was born. On our staff at Nopa, an intense young cook from Michoacán, Jose Ramos, had been producing insanely delicious meals (including a version of Nopalito's now-famous carnitas). Given Jose and Gonzalo's mutual love and knowledge of traditional Mexican cuisine, they formed a dynamic duo.

These two proud Mexican cooks, along with a couple of us hardworking gringos, opened Nopalito to much acclaim from our local San Franciscan foodies and quite a few nods from the national press. Three years later, the second location was built, and Gonzalo became the sole chef and creative force behind both restaurants.

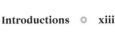

Gonzalo is one of my favorite humans—a great chef, an incredibly hard worker, a courageous and fiercely intelligent partner, and a close friend. Gonzo speaks from his heart and cooks from his soul. He is a dedicated partner, both to Jeff, Ally, and me, and to the mother of his two beautiful children. An honorable son, brother, cousin, and friend, Gonzalo brought along to our kitchens his cousins Lidia, Sergio, and Silverio, who have been with us from day one and to whom we also owe an incredible debt.

Over the last seven years, my understanding of Mexican cuisine has increased 1,000 percent, thanks to the Nopalito experience—and I know I'm not the only one who can say that. This is not boring or simple or expected food, and it's not food that falls back on stereotypes or clichés. The techniques are complex and labor intensive, and the menus achieve so many gutsy and delicious flavors using very simple ingredients and humble tradition-based recipes. As I've come to discover—and you will, too—chiles are not just about spice; they offer an array of flavors, from sweet and gentle to sour, charred, and smoky, and in some cases, yes, blow-your-head-off spicy. And the hard work required just to produce fresh masa alone—no doubt the core of Mexican cuisine, and one described so well in this book—means hours and hours of work at the restaurant scale. A cook with a traditional Western background simply couldn't imagine it.

Gonzalo has done an amazing job breaking down these recipes to make them accessible to the home cook. As you will see when you start to create these beautiful dishes yourself, much of the secret to their impact is in the layering of base flavors—the dish becoming the sum of all its parts, gaining something indispensable with each ingredient and each technique. This intensely seasoned, beautifully historic cooking humbles my "classically trained" palate. I have come to love everything about this cuisine.

I hope this book helps give you insight into the wonderful world of Mexican cooking and the beautiful people who interpret it daily at Nopalito.

Buen provecho.

—Laurence Jossel

Background and Basics:
From Mexico to Your Kitchen

IN THE MEXICAN KITCHEN

Many of the food traditions of Mexico historically revolved around three very simple pillars:

We ate mostly what we could grow ourselves.

We preserved what we grew, through drying, pickling, and other techniques.

We used all parts of everything we had access to, from the husks of the corn cobs to the fat from the animals.

We had little choice but to eat ingredients that were in season or to eat food that was grown locally. These options were based not on values but on necessity, as it was all many of us could afford. If you look at it this way, the key ingredients and ideas of Mexican cooking will seem like mostly common sense, and they are really not hard to understand or intimidating to master. Still, introducing them into your kitchen can open up a whole new world of flavors.

There are some cuisines that tout simplicity and integrity of ingredients as important above all else, and while Mexican ingredients may seem simplistic, what surprises many people about cooking authentic Mexican food is the intricacy, variety, and layers of flavor involved. For instance, the drying, then burning of chiles; the soaking and grinding of corn into masa; the blending of spices and herbs together to create a balanced salsa or mole—they all contribute to a nuanced and layered characteristic of the cuisine. Mexican food is, at heart, a labor-intensive style of cuisine from a hardworking people. To me, it is far too rare to see a restaurant or a home cook go the extra mile to transform simple ingredients, and that is why I felt inspired to open Nopalito—and to write this book.

Another part of the inspiration was to offer what I think is a glimpse into the true spirit, roots, and flavors of regional Mexican cooking. In the United States there is this idea that all Mexican meals start with chips and salsa, and that everything is laden with lard or cheese and comes with a side of rice and beans. But throughout my childhood in Mexico, our tables were spread with many dishes—most of them fresh, colorful, and inspired by what came straight from the sea and the land that day. The dishes that we ate in our homes every day are alive and well in these pages.

IN THE NOPALITO KITCHEN

When I first moved to San Francisco, I ate at one Mexican restaurant after another in search of something similar to the foods I grew up eating. I couldn't get used to the fact that everyone around me was buying premade tortillas in stores, or that burritos (which to me are not true Mexican food) seemed to dominate every menu.

When we decided to open Nopalito, it took me and my then co-chef months of thought and sourcing to figure out how to uphold all the from-scratch processes of authentic Mexican cooking that are so fundamental to the cuisine. We were obsessed with the idea of keeping things true to Mexico while making sure we were sourcing the best, most flavorful, and freshest local produce from California and nearby. I'm amazed we have been able to do so many of the things that are important to old-school Mexican cuisine, like grinding our own (always organic) corn from scratch every day, making queso fresco from scratch using local organic milk, and baking our own sandwich rolls in our restaurant kitchen each morning. It continues to mean eating by the seasons like we did in Mexico, and making sure our customers are too, never serving out-of-season tomatoes or subpar avocados just because people expect them on a Mexican menu.

Just as dishes with the same name in Mexico are made in a subtly different way in every home, town, and region, at Nopalito I have made some of my own adaptations and changes to traditional dishes to help make the best use of local ingredients and keep them up to the standards of the people of this wonderfully food-conscious region we live and work in, without misrepresenting the cuisine I grew up with. Whereas Mexicans often cook with a throw-everything-in-the-pot mentality, as a chef I can now apply some more thoughtful techniques to the cuisine of our grandmothers (and I don't think they would mind too much). Opening Nopalito was my first opportunity to really think about using chef techniques to embrace and enhance the nostalgic meals of Mexico.

It's funny to think I came all the way to Northern California only to end up doing what my mama did at home in Mexico. But I do pride myself in knowing that even if she were to walk through the door of Nopalito tomorrow, she would recognize every last dish from our menu, and most of the ingredients we are using. She, my *abuela*, and my brothers and sisters would see that the heart of our family cuisine is still intact in our restaurant kitchen. And, better yet, it is being shared with hundreds of people every day.

IN YOUR KITCHEN

There is no need to wait for a special moment to take out this cookbook and begin experimenting. Many of the recipes are designed for easy weeknight meals, or simple weekend breakfasts and brunches, or for whenever you're in the mood to whip up a Mexican-inspired snack or drink. Other recipes may take more time or steps, require a longer shopping list, or provide learning moments, but I have done my best to help you break down the steps as needed throughout the week, so serving becomes a matter of simply reheating and assembling. All of the dishes purposefully avoid fussiness or overdecoration, with the main focus being on deliciousness and authenticity. And the more familiar with the foundations you get, the easier the recipes will be.

This starts with understanding the essential ingredients of Mexican cooking.

BUILDING THE MEXICAN PANTRY

MASA:
THE HEART OF NOPALITO

In Mexico, each morning at 5:00 a.m., before the sun came up and the heat made it too difficult to do much of anything, my family and I would walk an hour and a half to our farm and tend to our fields of corn. Year-round we would harvest and dry the kernels, and each day grind them at the *molineria*—our communal corn grinder—in the center of town to make masa, which became the basis of all our meals.

Because of my upbringing in the south of Mexico, where the tropical weather makes corn one of the easiest crops to grow, I will always consider corn king of Mexican ingredients. As dramatic as it sounds, if I didn't have corn in my house in some form at all times, I don't think I would feel like a Mexican. At Nopalito, we cook between two hundred and three hundred pounds of corn a day, mostly in the form of masa. Masa is corn that has been treated to help remove its hulls, then ground into a doughy meal used to make tortillas and chips, thicken soups, and make countless other Mexican staples— huaraches (the dish, not the sandal), panuchos, tamales, and more. It is the basis of most dishes we serve at the restaurant and most of the recipes in this book.

The real mystery of masa is how something so simple can do so much and taste so good. While it may sound intimidating to make your own masa from scratch, most of the process is hands-off time, and you can find the raw ingredients online or at any Mexican market. Working with masa really is one of the more fun and rewarding parts of learning Mexican cuisine: feeling the soft dough between your fingers, pressing and flipping your first tortilla, and watching a tortilla puff up on the griddle.

Of course, there are shortcuts too, and we will get to those later. But whichever way you choose to prepare your masa, you will quickly realize it is well worth learning how to whip it up from time to time to create a delicious Mexican-inspired meal.

"NIXTAMALIZATION":
THE GATEWAY TO MASA

Masa is not made using corn kernels in their natural raw state. It begins with dried corn, which must first be *nixtamalized*—that is, soaked in an alkaline solution of calcium hydroxide (called "cal" for short), to loosen the hulls, soften the kernels, and make the kernels easier to grind and eat. Once the corn has been treated, we then call it *nixtamal*.

The nixtamalization process has been around for thousands of years. In ancient times, people used ashes from burnt wood to alkalize the corn, but today you can purchase cal online or in a Mexican market. The process may sound intimidating (and the word may look intimidating to pronounce), but making nixtamal is not difficult, and it is indispensable for making masa from scratch. Here are some general guidelines:

- Double-check your dried corn kernels by sorting through them as you would dried beans, checking for small pieces of stone or grit and discarding any you find.

- Get a head start by making nixtamal the day before you plan to cook with your masa. Nixtamal needs to soak for at least eight hours.

- While cal is technically safe to touch, like flour it can poof up into the air and cause some irritation in the eyes and throat if handled roughly.

- Be sure to measure masa ingredients rather than eyeballing them. Too much cal can give masa an off taste.

- Nixtamalization will double the size of the corn, so remember to account for this when choosing a mixing bowl.

- When rinsing the finished nixtamal, your hands should come out clean, with no skins from the corn remaining on your fingers. That is one way to tell that the nixtamalization is complete.

RED, BLUE, YELLOW, AND WHITE: CHOOSING A MASA

When it comes to choosing a corn color for masa, I believe in equal opportunity— I try to celebrate and use whatever corn is available to me. The main differences that distinguish white, yellow, red, and blue corn are merely small variations in the concentration of starches, sugars, and protein each variety contains. And, unless otherwise noted, they are interchangeable in these recipes.

If I *had* to rank them by color, I'd probably place blue corn at the top of the quality scale, by a slim margin, because it has a little more protein and less starch than the others, making it arguably healthier than the other corns and good for producing a smooth but sturdy masa. However, for the same reasons, blue corn is also more expensive and harder to find in large amounts. So you will more often see yellow or white available.

The differences between yellow and white corn are more subtle and seem to change depending on where the corn is grown and by whom, and which strain it is. There are no set rules for which corn you should use— you can more or less work with the colors interchangeably, and taste your way to your preferred choice.

One thing that is not so flexible: I always recommend seeking out top-quality, organic dried corn for the best flavor. When shopping, look for medium to medium-small kernels that are mostly unbroken, which will help them cook evenly.

6 cups (1½ quarts) dried corn (about 2½ pounds)

12 cups (3 quarts) water

3 tablespoons calcium hydroxide (cal)

To get the longest shelf life from masa, store it in a roomy container in the refrigerator. The cold will slow any fermentation that could render the masa sour. Take refrigerated masa out of the fridge 15 to 30 minutes before working with it. For best results, use it within the first 24 hours of grinding it. You'll need a corn grinder (see page 46) for this recipe.

HOMEMADE MASA

Makes enough for about 20 tortillas

In a large pot, combine the corn, water, and cal; bring to a boil, stirring occasionally. Let boil for 5 minutes, then turn off the heat. Let the corn sit overnight at room temperature, at least 8 hours and up to 16 hours (if using yellow corn, the corn will have turned more yellow).

Transfer to a colander and wash the corn under cold running water until all of the skins have come off and slipped away through the holes of the colander and the kernels look shiny.

Using a *molino de mano* (hand-cranked corn grinder like the one shown at right) or an electric corn grinder, grind the corn, pouring a little water over the corn as needed to get the mixture moving, and starting at a wide setting to help it slide through the grinder; as you continue, tighten the setting as much as you can. Repeat the grinding if necessary for a finer consistency. If making tortillas, you can grind the corn in a stone grinder (*metate*) to get an even more finely ground, smooth masa.

TIPS FOR PREPARING MASA
FROM STORE-BOUGHT
MASA HARINA

Almost any grocery store or health food store will carry masa harina, a flour made from ground nixtamalized corn, which can be turned instantly into masa by adding water. Because masa made this way will not have as much flavor (and definitely not as much texture) as masa made from home-ground nixtamal, I *always* suggest and prefer the made-from-scratch version.

If you do plan to use the store-bought option, however, follow the directions on the back of the package, following these tips for best results:

- Be sure to season masa harina with a little salt to help bring out the flavor in the corn and prevent blandness.

- When mixing masa from harina, start with a little less than the recommended amount of water. Too-wet masa can be very soft and difficult to work with, and it won't have as fluffy and springy a consistency. Reserve a few tablespoons of liquid when initially combining the ingredients, and add them only if needed. Let the masa rest for at least 10 minutes (some packages recommend up to an hour) to absorb the water before adding more. The finished product should be the consistency of moist, smooth mashed potatoes, or a soft, fluffy sugar cookie dough.

- If masa is dry or crumbly while working with it, mix in a bit more water.

- Store extra masa in the refrigerator (one to two days maximum) to help keep it from fermenting or turning sour. Let chilled masa come to room temperature for 15 to 30 minutes before working with it.

HOW TO MAKE SOFT CORN TORTILLAS

You can do so many things with simple corn tortillas, from sautéing them as a base for breakfast chilaquiles to turning them into crispy chips or *totopos* to using them for tacos, enchiladas, and many more *antojitos* (small plates or street foods).

Making perfectly round and evenly thick tortillas is a skill that will improve with practice. But the good news is, even an imperfectly shaped tortilla can still be incredibly delicious. You will achieve the thinnest, most consistent tortillas by using a tortilla press. I prefer and recommend the wooden or metal versions. Here's how to make a tortilla both with and without a press.

WITH A TORTILLA PRESS: Line the bottom of a tortilla press with a round of plastic, cut from a plastic bag. For a 6-inch tortilla, form about 3 tablespoons of masa into a ball, then flatten the ball slightly into a disk. Place the disk atop the plastic-lined tortilla press. Line the top with another round of plastic. Lower the top half and press down on the handle, distributing your weight evenly across the press. Open the press and carefully separate the tortilla from the plastic. Preheat a griddle or skillet to medium heat and quickly wipe or drizzle the surface with a little oil. Add the tortilla and cook until slightly dried, about 60 seconds. Continue to flip every 30 to 60 seconds until cooked through and puffing up with air, about 3 minutes total. (Do not overcook, as this can toughen the tortilla.)

WITHOUT A TORTILLA PRESS: Sandwich the masa round between two pieces of cut-out plastic on a clean work surface. Use the underside of a flat-bottomed plate, bowl, or pan to press and flatten the masa into a very thin round.

TO MAKE CHILE-FLAVORED TORTILLAS: Add 3 ancho chiles to a heatproof bowl; cover with boiling water and let sit until very soft, about 20 minutes. Drain the chiles (reserve the soaking water) and transfer to a blender; blend, adding a little of the soaking water only as necessary to form a thick paste. Let cool completely. Place 2½ cups masa in a medium bowl and add some of the cooled chile paste until you've reached a heat level you like, mixing with your hands and tasting as you go. Follow the preceding instructions for shaping your tortillas.

STORING AND USING YOUR HOMEMADE TORTILLAS

If you have made tortillas using your own masa and plan to serve them later that day, as soon as you remove each hot tortilla from the griddle, transfer it straight to a plastic bag while they are still hot (you can stack them, then seal the bag), and then transfer to the refrigerator. When ready to eat, quickly reheat them on a dry, medium-heat griddle.

MORE WAYS TO USE YOUR MASA

Soft Corn Tortillas for Quesadillas

You are probably used to making quesadillas by sandwiching fillings between two round tortillas, right? In Mexico it is more common to fill one larger, oval-shaped tortilla with cheese and other ingredients, then fold it in half atop the griddle (they turn out looking a little like a slightly longer version of a soft taco). The bonus is, you can easily flip them without the filling falling out the sides of the shells.

Crispy Corn Tostadas

These crispy shells are placed on the bottom of the plate and often spread with a layer of refried beans and piled high with toppings. The corn tortillas are dried out slightly and rendered crispy through baking or frying (see page 117).

Corn Tortilla Chips

Frying tortilla chips, or *totopos*, from scratch (see page 66) yields a thicker, sturdier chip that has a more pronounced corn flavor. It also means you can control the level of salt on your chips. For best results, start with homemade tortillas between one and four days old. The extra time dries them out slightly, preventing them from turning out too greasy when fried. Or, in a pinch, use store-bought corn tortillas right from the package.

Fried Empanadas

Empanadas are savory or sweet pies stuffed with a variety of fillings, like vegetables, seafood, or meat, depending where you are in Mexico. Sweet ones are typically made with flour-based pastry. But where I'm from, they are always fried and made with masa pastry.

Tamales

A dish from ancient Mexico, tamales at their simplest consist of well-seasoned masa steamed inside a corn husk, banana leaf, or other wrapper. In many cases, the masa also encases shredded or chopped meats, vegetables, chicken, or beans. The trick to making tender tamales is to moisten the masa well with either lard or softened unsalted butter, or even a little extra water or cooking stock.

Huaraches

A huarache is a Mexican street food that uses a bed of masa pressed slightly thicker than a tortilla, in the shape of a shoe sole (*huarache* means "sandal" in Spanish). You can distribute toppings like shredded stewed meats or sautéed vegetables on top, and garnish as you like (see page 114).

Gorditas

A gordita is a miniature sandwich made by splitting a lightly crispy corn masa cake down the center and stuffing it with savory fillings (similar to how you would stuff a pita bread). One makes a great snack and two make a nice meal. (See page 113 for how to form and cook gorditas.)

Panuchos

Like a cross between a tostada and a gordita, a panucho is a crispy little masa cake that is split open in the center and filled with beans. After filling and closing up the panucho, you then pile toppings on its outer layer (much as you would do with a tostada).

I will always be partial to corn tortillas; they have a bit more texture and flavor than their wheat-based counterparts, plus you can transform them into all sorts of other treats like corn chips, chilaquiles, and tostadas. But there is a time and a place for flour tortillas, and they are very popular in the cuisine from the northern states of Mexico. This is Nopalito's recipe, which makes a large, thin but fluffy flour tortilla.

TORTILLAS DE HARINA

Wheat Flour Tortillas ○ Makes 16

4 cups all-purpose flour, plus more for rolling

4½ tablespoons lard or softened unsalted butter

1½ teaspoons kosher salt

1½ teaspoons baking powder

1¼ cups plus 2 tablespoons warm water

In a stand mixer fitted with the paddle attachment, beat the flour, lard, salt, and baking powder until combined. Slowly trickle in the water with the motor running, beating until just incorporated and an elastic dough forms.

Portion the dough into ¼-cup (2-ounce) balls and set on a baking sheet. Cover the sheet with plastic wrap and place in a warm place to rest for 1 hour. The dough will increase in size.

Lightly flour a clean work surface. Work with one ball at a time and keep the remaining balls covered while you work. Place the ball between two pieces of plastic wrap and, using a rolling pin, roll it out into a thin round about 9 inches in diameter. While you are rolling out the tortillas, heat a large skillet or griddle to medium heat and add the tortillas one at a time; cook, turning once, until no longer raw-looking and blistered slightly, about 2 minutes on each side. Remove and let cool, then cover with plastic wrap until ready to use.

BEYOND MASA: MEXICAN PANTRY ESSENTIALS

There is a small set of modest ingredients required for most of the recipes in this book. Some of them may be new to your kitchen—in which case, you have much to look forward to—and all of them are very affordable, easy to work with, and usually fairly easy to find. The majority of ingredients can be purchased at basic grocery stores, and others can most certainly be found online or in a Mexican market. Having just a few of them on hand at any time will put most of the recipes in this book at your fingertips.

Dried Chiles

There is a reason Mexican markets often give dried chiles a larger display than any other ingredient. They are Mexican cuisine's steady workhorses, appearing in so many of the traditional dishes—including many of the ones in this book. When I first moved to California, I was surprised to see that at Mexican restaurants here, the most attention is paid to fresh chiles like jalapeños, serranos, habaneros, and poblanos. These are wonderful too, but it is the dried chiles that offer the most surprising and complex flavors in Mexican cooking—from smoky to spicy to chocolaty, earthy, and mushroomy. You won't believe the array until you have tried them all yourself.

One of the most common ways we use dried Mexican chiles in this book is to blend them into *adobo*, a generic term for a paste, marinade, sauce, or seasoning made by reconstituting dried chiles, then pureeing them. There are many variations on adobo, since they may feature individual chiles or a combination of them, plus a variety of spices, herbs, aromatics, vinegar, and other seasonings. Since a few dried chiles have thick, bitter, or very spicy seeds, we will occasionally suggest removing the seeds from some of them before using. To do this, simply snap off the stem end or split the chile flesh lengthwise with the tip of a paring knife, then shake the chile to dislodge and remove the seeds. You can make adobo up to a few days in advance and store it refrigerated in a sealed container.

The same way you can walk through the potato bins at the market and easily distinguish the russets from the sweet potatoes, you will soon be able to spot the differences between types of dried chiles.

In the meantime, use this cheat sheet to help choose the right chiles for the job.

Dried Red Chiles

Red chiles typically have bright colors, tropical fruit flavors, a good amount of acidity, and varying degrees of spice. They pair best with poultry, fish, and other light or lean meats. The following are ranked from mildest to hottest.

GUAJILLO o **Bright red, large and skinny, tough skins, sweet but with some acidity, relatively mild heat**

Tips for using: Guajillos are used frequently throughout this book, possibly more than any other dried chile. They are also very popular in Mexico. The reason is their crowd-pleasing flavor—a mix of earthy and sweet, and typically little to no heat. But they are usually a larger pepper, so a few go a long way to add thickness and body to adobos, stews, and sauces. Guajillos combine well with other chiles and tomatoes without overpowering them with spice or smokiness. Because of their thin but tough skins, they need 20 to 25 minutes of soaking time in boiling water when reconstituting from dried.

PUYA o **Similar to guajillos but smaller and spicier, earthy, fruity but with some acidity, medium heat**

Tips for using: The puya is basically a smaller, spicier version of the guajillo. Puya chiles are bright red with a thin but tough skin like their big brother, and because they are quite dry, puyas take well to toasting. Once they've been toasted, you can cool them and grind them into a chili powder for sprinkling onto foods to add a dose of heat. You can use puyas in any preparations in which you would use guajillos, including stews, braises, and sauces, if you are looking to boost the spiciness. Just add them a little at a time and taste, so as not to overdo it.

CHIPOTLE o **Medium sized, tough skinned, smoky, medium heat**

Tips for using: The chipotle is actually a smoked, dried version of one of Mexico's most common chiles, the jalapeño. They are red because they are picked at the end of the ripening process.

Chipotles have a medium heat, and are known for their distinct smokiness and earthy flavor. I like to use chipotles for making table salsas, as well as Chipotles Adobados (page 42)—reconstituted chipotles served in

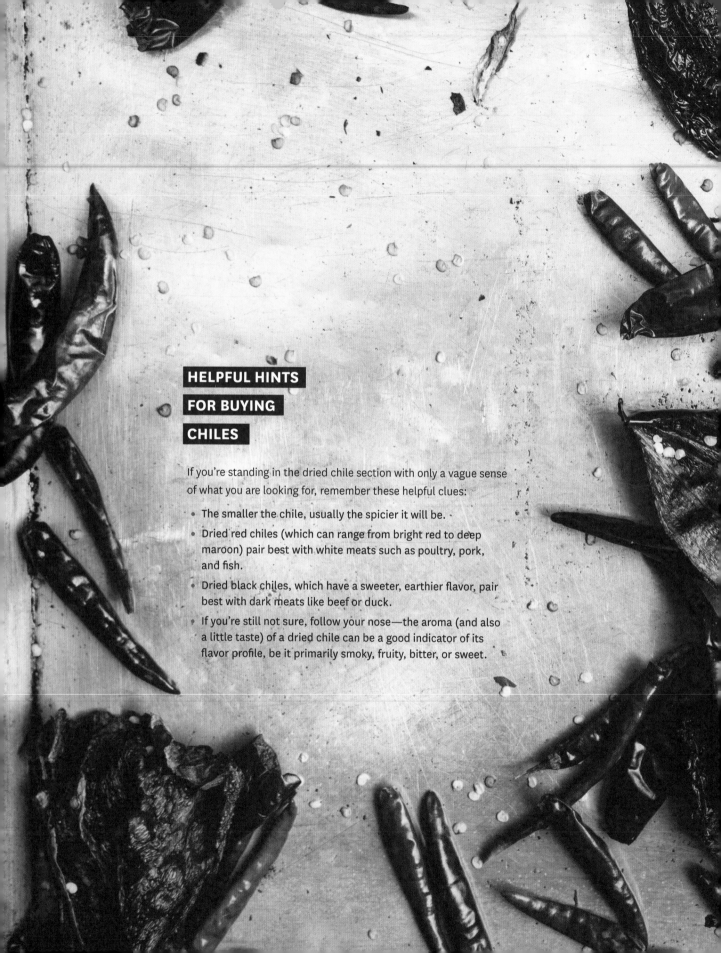

HELPFUL HINTS
FOR BUYING
CHILES

If you're standing in the dried chile section with only a vague sense of what you are looking for, remember these helpful clues:

- The smaller the chile, usually the spicier it will be.
- Dried red chiles (which can range from bright red to deep maroon) pair best with white meats such as poultry, pork, and fish.
- Dried black chiles, which have a sweeter, earthier flavor, pair best with dark meats like beef or duck.
- If you're still not sure, follow your nose—the aroma (and also a little taste) of a dried chile can be a good indicator of its flavor profile, be it primarily smoky, fruity, bitter, or sweet.

a rich chile paste that is often blended into braising liquids or marinades. By simply soaking chipotles in boiling water, then blending with a few tomatillos, you can have a simple medium-heat salsa to dip your chips in.

CHILE DE ÁRBOL ○ Small, nutty, earthy, very spicy

Tips for using: You might think I'm crazy to be in love with a chile, but believe me, the chile de árbol (or árbol chile) is not like other chiles. This is probably my go-to red chile for making table salsas as well as salsas *taqueras* (a generic term we use in Mexico for salsas that go well with tacos). The árbol is a chameleon, changing depending on how it is handled—toasting and frying it intensifies its heat and nutty qualities. But however you cook it, its slender fruit packs a big punch in both spice and earthy flavor. Look for chiles de árbol with stems (rather than crushed or preground) for the best flavor.

PEQUIN ○ Tiny, a little smoky, a little fruity, very spicy

Tips for using: Also called the bird chile, the pequins are tiny chiles that will shock you with their spiciness. They are great for a sharp salsa taquera, and we also use them as the basis for our house hot sauce (page 234), combining them with vinegar and tomato paste to tame some of the heat and add sweetness.

MORITA ○ Petite, smoky, sweet dried-fruit flavors, medium to high heat

Tips for using: Chiles moritas are small but substantial chiles that I always like to have in my house. They add both smokiness and a decent amount of heat to salsas and sauces. Because of their dried fruit–like sweetness, plus the fact that they can be quite spicy, they fall somewhere between red and dark chiles. I like to add them to dark moles such as mole poblano or Oaxacan-style moles to give them a little heat without taking away from their dark color.

Dark Chiles

Dark chiles, which are usually a deep purple and sometimes fully black, tend to have a chewier, more moist texture and the sweet flavors of very ripe dried fruits like raisins and prunes. Not many of them are very spicy—they are used more for their color, sweetness, and sometimes smokiness. The following are ranked from mildest to spiciest.

CHILE NEGRO (also called pasilla negro, pasilla chile, or chile Oaxaca) ○ Large and long, with earthiness, mellow dried-fruit flavors (raisins, prunes), mild heat

Tips for using: This chile is very dark, nearly black, and used frequently in making mole negro. The chile negro is used and loved more for its color than for its flavor, since its taste and heat level are relatively mild.

MULATO ○ Sweet, lightly smoky, dried-fruit flavors (raisins, prunes), mild heat

Tips for using: Mulatos, like anchos, are a relative of the poblano chile, and have a similar smoky-sweet profile, especially when charred. However, they are darker than anchos, with a brownish-purple tinge. Mulatos are a thick, meaty chile, so they make a great addition to moles, pozoles, and other dishes where they can be blended into an adobo or paste to add body, intense fruit flavors, and dark colors to a dish.

CASCABEL ○ Round, tropical, fruity (dried apricots, dried apples), relatively mild heat

Tips for using: The cascabel is a very round, hollow chile. Its name comes from the Spanish word for "rattle" (it is shaped like the end of a rattlesnake's tail, and the seeds noisily rattle around inside the dried chile when it is shaken). It is a very aromatic chile, without much heat but with an intense fruity, tropical flavor. If you want flavor over heat, the cascabel is a good choice.

ANCHO ○ Ripe-fruit flavors, lightly smoky, mildly spicy

Tips for using: The ancho chile is actually a poblano chile that has been ripened to a deep red, then picked and dried. Its spice level fluctuates depending on the individual chile, but in general the ancho has mild to moderate heat. Anchos are particularly good for marinating meats as part of an adobo, or you can stir some ancho adobo into masa to give a small kick of heat and beautiful dark red color.

PASILLA ○ Complex, dried fruits (raisins, prunes), medium spicy

Tips for using: The pasilla is named after the word for "raisins" (*pasas*) on account of its deeply sweet dried fruit flavors and wrinkly, dark appearance. Compared to the ancho, the pasilla's texture is a bit tougher, and its heat more intense. I like to combine it with mulatos and a few dried red chiles in Oaxacan-style moles to create a perfect blend of color, sweetness, and mild spice.

Nopales and Nopalitos

I think everyone is equal parts intimidated and excited when they pick up a fresh cactus leaf for the first time. These bright green paddles (*nopales* are the slightly larger paddles, and *nopalitos* are the littler ones) are hacked from the prickly pear cactus plant and naturally have a sweet, vegetal flavor somewhat similar to a green bean with the texture of a succulent plant. They need their pointy spines scraped off with a sharp knife, but don't worry—many stores will have already done this part for you. If you have to do it yourself, quickly run a sharp, heavy knife underneath the base of each spine, trimming it away.

You can grill nopales, sear them on a *comal* or skillet, eat them raw as a snack or in salads, cure them with salt, or even puree them into smoothies. They can have a bit of a slimy texture when cooked, but salting them in advance and letting some of their liquid drain out should help with this. Nopales can be found at some farmers' markets or grocery stores and almost any Mexican market. Look for nopales that feel firm and are bright green, and try to use them within a day or two so they retain their full snap and color.

Annatto Seeds (Achiote)

Basically a natural food dye, annatto seeds come from a little shrub that grows in Central and South America. You can find them at many gourmet grocery stores or any spice shop. Typically the whole seeds are soaked in water, then ground into a paste (called *achiote* in Mexico, which is why you might sometimes see annatto seeds labeled as achiote), but you can also buy annatto as a preground spice. The seeds add a bright yellow-orange color—most famously to the Yucatán pork dish cochinita—but they don't have much flavor. The exception is when they are used in large amounts, at which point at most you will detect a faintly bitter, earthy quality.

Piloncillo

Piloncillo is unrefined pure cane juice that is molded into cones and sold in bulk bins at Mexican markets. It has a more complex flavor than regular cane sugar, with some deeper caramel notes, and in Mexico it is used in both sweet and savory preparations. (I love it in carnitas to give that lightly sweet barbecue taste.) You can buy piloncillo in 3-, 7-, 8-, or 12-ounce cones. For some dishes

the cone is thrown into the pot whole and allowed to melt. But since the cones can be very hard to measure or reduce into smaller amounts, you will need to carefully grate the cone on the large-holed side of a box grater or a *molcajete* (mortar); this may require a little muscle. You can substitute brown sugar for piloncillo if needed, but since brown sugar has added molasses, the flavor and consistency will be a bit different.

Hominy

If you recall learning about nixtamal (page 7), hominy will be an easy concept for you. Hominy essentially *is* nixtamal—corn kernels that have been soaked in an alkaline solution to strip away their hulls and protein germs. The kernels puff up to triple the size of regular corn kernels, making them fluffy, chewy, and pleasantly starchy. They retain their sweetness but also take on a nutty, popcorn-like flavor. We use cooked hominy to thicken and bulk up our pozole and some other soups and stews. You can buy it canned at most grocery stores, but the home-cooked version has a richer flavor.

Banana Leaves

Because banana leaves tend to lose freshness quickly, the freezer section at a Mexican market is the best place to look for them. They have several uses in Mexican cooking, but most often you will use banana leaves as a wrap or shell in which to cook and lightly flavor other foods. Since they fold easily, we will use them to wrap tamale filling or pieces of fish, then either steam or cook them atop a griddle or skillet, where the heat can penetrate through, cook the foods inside, and lend foods a grassy sweetness. Because of their sturdy waxy consistency, banana leaves help protect food while it cooks and lock in its juices. We also use banana leaves to flavor roasted or braised meats. The leaves themselves are never eaten.

Lard

Lard gets a bad rap here in the States, but in Mexico it has long been embraced as a go-to fat for griddling foods such as antojitos on the comal. To most Mexicans it is also the only true fat to use for traditional refried beans. Lard is rendered pork fat, so it is best purchased fresh (not packaged or hydrogenated) at butcher shops or Mexican grocers, where it will usually have a light tan color and slightly meaty smell. At Nopalito and in Mexico, lard adds flavor and moisture to our masa for tamales. But for vegetarian dishes or if you can't find fresh lard, you can substitute softened unsalted butter where specified.

Avocado Leaves

It is worth your while to seek out avocado leaves, which are typically sold dried—or, if you're lucky, occasionally fresh—at Mexican markets. They are a little larger than bay leaves but similar in the ways they are used: adding one or two to a stew, meat braising liquid, or pot of beans will impart a subtle anise flavor for which there really is no substitute. We have made avocado leaves optional in the recipes in this book, but if you can find them, their unique flavor is worth pursuing. Everyone will want to know the secret ingredient in your recipe.

Mexican Chocolate

Nowadays there are many quality types of chocolate available at almost any grocery store in the United States. But Mexican chocolate is its own style entirely, and really should not be substituted for in these recipes. Portioned into circular disks, Mexican chocolate is a bitter, medium-dark chocolate that has been seasoned with cinnamon and coarse grains of sugar, so it has a rougher texture than other chocolates. Since each brand is unique, we recommend you buy either Ibarra or Abuelita brand to achieve consistency in recipes. Mexican chocolate is great to have around the house for making a mug of hot chocolate or melting into a mole.

Huitlacoche

It is not going to sound glamorous when I tell you what huitlacoche is, but it is a delicacy in Mexico and, I would say, a food worth checking off from your bucket list. Huitlacoche (or "corn smut") is a rare fungus that grows naturally—but randomly—on corn crops. Out of hundreds of corn plants, maybe only one will have it, so we call it the truffle of Mexico. It has a blue-black color and a mushroomy flavor. You will usually find it frozen at Mexican markets. Use huitlacoche as a filling or topping for antojitos, such as quesadillas or huaraches (page 114).

Tomatillos

A little bit tart, and highly acidic, these plump green cousins of the tomato are otherwise relatively mild flavored. Tomatillos are sometimes boiled or roasted to sweeten them up a bit, or you can puree them raw and mix them with nothing more than some white onion, garlic, cilantro, and/or jalapeño to turn them into an instant salsa verde. They really come to life with a little salt and some lime juice. When shopping, remember that smaller, lighter-colored tomatillos will have more acid, and the larger, darker green fruits tend to be a little sweeter. Remember to remove their husks before using, and wash the fruits thoroughly to remove any stickiness.

Epazote

Epazote is a resinous Mexican herb that grows predominantly in the tropical south of the country. I have a hard time describing it. It has a strong, herbaceous flavor that's like mint, oregano, and anise combined—some might describe it as soapy or medicinal. It was one of the only flavorings used in the traditional bean dishes in Mexico, and it goes well with other earthy foods such as huitlacoche or mushrooms, stews, and tamales.

Queso Oaxaca

This white semihard cheese is probably most comparable to a Jack or mozzarella cheese—it shreds and strings easily and has a mild flavor. It is named after the region where it was first made, where it is used frequently to make quesadillas, tortas, and *tlayudas*, a large, crispy fried tortilla with layers of toppings.

Queso Cotija

Cotija is a very crumbly cheese with a high salt content and a somewhat aged taste—most similar to ricotta salata. In the small towns of Mexico, we made our cheese from scratch every day (see Queso Fresco, page 32), so we favored that style a bit more than Cotija for topping totopos or antojitos. But nowadays Cotija is usually fairly easy to find in grocery stores and makes a good option for garnishing.

Other Commonly Used Ingredients

TOMATOES ◦ Tomatoes are an essential ingredient in many raw, cooked, and fried salsas (*salsas fritas*) in Mexico. They also turn up in stews, *adobos* (chile pastes), braised meats, and ceviches. Buy them firm-ripe in the summer and early fall, or stick to canned diced tomatoes (with their liquid—never drained) in the off seasons.

TOMATO PASTE ◦ This concentrated form of tomatoes comes in handy when you need to quickly add some deep sweetness to braises, adobos, and salsas.

OREGANO ◦ Mexicans use this herb generously, both fresh and dried. If you can find it, Mexican oregano has a slightly more pungent flavor and larger, broader leaves than Mediterranean or European oregano.

MARJORAM ◦ This is oregano's more delicate cousin. If you can't find it readily, just use oregano.

CILANTRO ◦ In my opinion, you can never have too much cilantro in your house. We use the leaves and sometimes even a little of the stems as a fresh garnish or stir them into salsas to add a bright, grassy note. You can also add cilantro to stocks or braises, or blend it into an adobo. Its flavor is not as strong when cooked or mixed with other strong flavors.

CLOVES ◦ Found in the spice section, these tiny, aromatic dried flower buds of the clove tree are used a lot in Mexican cooking. Their woodsy, perfume-y, and slightly sweet aroma and flavor are assertive, so a little goes a long way when you're making rich stews, braises, chorizo, salsas, or desserts.

CORN HUSKS ◦ Used to make tamales, these usually come in a bag with a mix of large and small husks. For the greatest ease filling and forming them, first soak them in hot water for twenty minutes, then use all the large husks first. Lay the smaller ones side by side lengthwise to give yourself more area to work with.

BAY LEAF ◦ Fine to buy fresh or dried, bay leaves can impart a complex herbal flavor to stews, braises, soups, and stocks. Many braised or simmered meats in this book are flavored simply by adding bay leaves and white onion to the cooking liquid.

CUMIN ◦ Available in seed form or ground, cumin is popular in Mexican dishes; its strong, nutty-peppery flavor and aroma are great on meats and in dried chile salsas. If using whole seeds, toast them in a dry skillet or roast in a 350°F oven on a baking sheet for a few minutes to intensify their flavor before grinding.

DRIED BEANS ◦ The beans we use most at Nopalito are black beans, pinto beans or pinquito beans (a smaller variety of pink beans that are a little smaller than pinto), and butter beans. We source our beans through Rancho Gordo, which grows high-quality heirloom beans locally in California. Most often we serve braised or refried beans as a side dish.

WHITE ONIONS ◦ I'm not sure why Mexicans favor these onions more than other onions. Perhaps it is their clean, sharp flavor. Garnishing with finely chopped or thinly sliced white onions helps to cut through and balance fatty meats, cheeses, or other rich foods.

RED ONIONS ◦ Red onions are a popular garnish on Mexican antojitos, soups, and stews. They are especially good for cutting through fatty dishes, and they go equally well with hearty meats and white fish. I prefer them to white onions as a garnish whenever I need to add a dose of flavor and a little sweetness along with a sharp onion flavor.

AVOCADOS ◦ There is nothing quite like a ripe avocado to add creaminess, coolness, and contrast to a dish. We love them especially atop an antojito or ceviche, and of course mashed up into guacamole.

MEXICAN CHORIZO ◦ This spicy fresh pork sausage is probably the most popular in Mexican cuisine, and it has also become quite common in the United States. Mexican-style chorizo is usually raw, which means it must be cooked before eating, and in recipes it is often used out of its casing, crumbled into the pan. I prefer to make my own chorizo so I can control the seasonings (see recipe on page 44).

AGAVE NECTAR ◦ Extracted from the same plant as tequila, agave nectar is sold bottled as a runny syrup at almost any grocery store here in the States. Like honey, the thicker and less refined, the better. At Nopalito, we use it to sweeten drinks because it dissolves more quickly than cane sugar, and you can instantly turn it into a syrup by mixing with equal parts water. Sugar is a fine substitute if you don't have agave nectar on hand.

GREEN CABBAGE ○ I always have a head of crunchy green cabbage on hand for topping *tortas* and *cemitas* (Mexican sandwiches), making into an easy salad or slaw, or garnishing an antojito or stew. In Mexico, a simple cabbage salad made with lime juice and salt is classic alongside big-batch meats, like carnitas.

VEGETABLE OIL ○ For most everyday kitchen tasks, I prefer rice bran oil or canola oil for their clean flavors and high smoke points (that is, their ability to cook foods at really high temperatures without burning, smoking, or becoming bitter). To me, rice bran oil is a little lighter and leaves less grease on foods when fried, so I give it a slight edge over canola. But if you can't find rice bran, canola is a good substitute.

PEPITAS ○ Pepitas are pumpkin seeds, and when we call for them in this book we mean the hulled, raw, and ideally organic version that can be found in any health food store and most grocery stores. We toast them either in the oven or in a dry skillet on the stove top to give them more crunch and bring out their oils and flavors. They are used in some salsas as well as in *pipiáns*—traditional sauces and moles that vary through the regions but always contain ground seeds or nuts.

GARLIC ○ Your old friend garlic certainly has a place in Mexican cuisine. It is usually a background flavor, often blended raw or roasted into salsas. I also usually toss in a few cloves when I braise a whole chicken or a large cut of pork.

LIMES AND LEMONS ○ Limes and lemons can be a little confusing when you're going from Spanish to English. In many parts of Mexico, the word *limón*, which sounds a lot like "lemon," actually means "lime." In other parts of Mexico, they use the word *lima*. In Spanish, I generally call what Americans know as "limes," *limones* verdes or *limones verdes pequeños*. And there are even more terms for limes than that: *limon amarillo*, *limon criollo*, and other names for particular fruits used in particular regions.

In many parts of Mexico, the lemon is not widely used, or used at all. Where I'm from we did use yellow lemons, but because they are slightly sweeter in southern Mexico, we mainly used them for agua frescas.

For the purposes of this book, the word *lemon* means the yellow fruit as we know it in America. And *lime* means the green.

Limes are our favorite way to add a kick of acidity and sweetness to a dish, or counterbalance the effect of something very spicy. Because their flavor, acidity, intensity, and even juice content can vary through the seasons and from batch to batch, we always suggest tasting the dish and adjusting the amount of lime juice needed to find the right balance of flavors. On average, a plump, juicy lime will yield about 1 ounce of juice.

JALAPEÑOS ○ There is hardly a time that a Mexican cook won't have this fresh chile on hand. We called it the *chile de amor* because it is our beloved staple. The jalapeño tastes delicious both raw and cooked and is used in many salsas and ceviches and with meats served "à la Mexicana" (a classic preparation that features tomatoes, onions, and jalapeños). In many parts of the country, Mexicans will even griddle jalapeños until their outsides became charred, then take bites straight from the whole chile in between bites of the meal. Jalapeños vary greatly in spiciness, so be sure to taste yours for spice before deciding on the quantity to add. Cooking it will usually dull its heat, or you can seed fresh chiles if you have a low spice tolerance.

SERRANOS ○ Spicier than a jalapeño, a little fresh serrano can go a long way. I like to use thinly sliced raw serranos as a garnish to add crunch and heat to a finished dish. Seeding them helps tame the burn.

HABANEROS ○ Mexicans like everything spicy, so having salsa made with fresh habaneros is pretty much a must at every kiosk or antojito vendor around town (see our recipe for Habanero Salsa on page 221). They are particularly obsessed with habaneros in the Yucatán, where many of the local salsas contain this fruity, tropical, and highly spicy chile. Habaneros are small and physically delicate, but they pack a mighty punch. We recommend using gloves to handle them, or at least thoroughly washing your hands and avoiding touching your eyes or face after working with them.

HOJA SANTA ○ I grew up in a house in Mexico surrounded by hoja santa plants. The leaves—commonly used in Oaxacan moles—add a really strong, pleasantly bitter flavor to dishes, much like avocado leaves do. However, hoja santa is a large plant, producing leaves about three times the size. You will really taste the impact of one on a dish. If you can find the leaves fresh, a traditional way to use them is to blend them into masa, then stir the seasoned masa into mole. Dried, you can use them like bay leaves.

A FEW HOUSE RECIPES

Having spent my early years picking whatever produce I needed from my family's garden, or the farms nearby, you might say I am a little choosy about freshness. My cooks at Nopalito know I will always go the extra mile to start and end my recipes with the best ingredients. This includes making fundamentals like stocks, condiments, and even breads from scratch, many of them on a daily basis.

What might be considered as more work at first glance can easily become second-nature once you see that the difference in flavor is worth it. When you've tasted how good fluffy, fresh torta or cemita rolls can be for sandwiches, or how much more moist and light—not dried out—homemade queso fresco can be, you will be not only willing but excited to incorporate these staples into your kitchen repertoire. The good news is, many of the recipes in this section last a significant amount of time in your refrigerator or freezer. Spending ten minutes to make one batch of *jalapeños curtidos* (pickled jalapeños) or *escabeche rojo* (pickled red onions) can give you a month or more worth of accompaniments for tacos, brunch dishes, and dinners.

Of course, it's not about having quality ingredients around, but also what you do with them, that makes the best-tasting Mexican food. Start with just a few of these recipes to stock your refrigerator and pantry, then use them again and again to cook your way through the classic Mexican dishes in this book.

I am a bit picky when it comes to the quality of ingredients, which is why everything we serve at Nopalito—from the torta rolls to the hot sauce—is made from scratch, using the most responsibly farmed, local ingredients possible. These staple-dish components couldn't be simpler to put together, and you will reach for them again and again in your everyday cooking.

Queso fresco, a fresh cheese that's mild like ricotta but has a slightly firmer consistency, is my favorite Mexican cheese, and the type we probably use most at Nopalito. After a lifetime of making it fresh, I am not very fond of the store-bought versions. Some brands are too creamy, others too dry, others too rubbery—and they don't taste as natural. Luckily, the process of making your own queso fresco couldn't be simpler, as long as you have a deep-fat thermometer.

In addition to crumbling queso fresco atop almost any antojito, sandwich, or side of beans, you can chop this cheese into bite-sized pieces and add it to the bottom of bowls of soup before ladling in the broth. The cheese becomes warm and soft as it sits, and it also helps to make the soup more filling.

QUESO FRESCO

Makes 3 cups

12 cups (¾ gallon) organic whole milk

1¼ cups distilled white vinegar

3 teaspoons kosher salt

In a large pot, heat the milk over medium-high heat, stirring often, until a thermometer reads 170°F. Pour in the vinegar and, using a wooden spoon, stir for 2 minutes to allow the milk to curdle. (The curds will appear small.) Turn off the heat and let sit for 20 minutes.

Line the inside of a strainer with enough cheesecloth to drape over the sides of the strainer by a few inches, then place the strainer in the sink. Carefully pour the cheese mixture into the prepared strainer; let sit until the liquid is mostly drained out. Bring the open ends of the cheesecloth together in your hands to form a bundle, then squeeze out any remaining liquid. Place the bundle back in the strainer.

Set the strainer inside a bowl to continue draining, and place some weight on top of the cheese. Let rest and cool for 1 hour.

Unwrap the cheesecloth and sprinkle the cheese with the salt; stir or toss to distribute evenly. Close up the cheesecloth and place the weight back on top. Refrigerate for at least 8 hours or up to overnight.

Remove the cheesecloth and discard. The cheese will be ready to crumble or dice. Store in an airtight wrap or container and refrigerate for up to 10 days.

Ground dried chiles and lime juice is a classic seasoning combination in Mexico—almost everybody has dried chili powder at home to sprinkle on fruits. I do it with oranges or watermelon in my own kitchen or any fresh fruit salad on our menu at the restaurant. The preground chili powders sold in grocery stores just don't hold a candle to the flavor of chiles you toast and grind yourself, which is why we insist upon making our own at the restaurant using a combination of árbol chiles (for heat) and guajillo chiles (for volume and sweetness). We have found so many uses for this combination—from serving it on fried chickpeas as a table snack to making spiced nuts for salads—that we named it our house spice.

NOPALITO SPICES

Makes about ¾ cup

1 ounce dried árbol chiles (1¼ cups, about 50 small chiles), stemmed and seeded

1 ounce dried guajillo chiles (1¼ cups, about 6 chiles), stemmed and seeded

Preheat the oven to 350°F. Place all of the chiles on a small baking sheet or large ovenproof skillet and transfer to the oven. Cook, turning the peppers every minute or so, until darkened and evenly toasted, 3 to 8 minutes (the timing will vary depending on the heat of your pan and the individual chiles). Remove and let cool completely.

Transfer the chiles to a blender and grind into a powder, using a scraper or small rubber spatula to direct the chiles toward the blade (alternatively, grind in batches using a spice grinder). Store in an airtight container.

Crema is a staple on Mexican tables. It is a thick, cultured cream seasoned with salt and thinned with a little lime juice for added tartness. We use Greek yogurt as the base of our crema at Nopalito—its added tanginess helps to cool the mouth and contrast with some of the spicier ingredients that may be on the plate.

CREMA

Makes 1 cup

1 cup plain whole-milk Greek yogurt

3 teaspoons freshly squeezed lime juice

½ teaspoon kosher salt, or more to taste

In a small bowl, combine the yogurt, lime juice, and salt and stir well. Thin with a little water if necessary. Taste and adjust the lime juice and salt as needed.

Teleras are the most common rolls for tortas in Mexico. They are usually round and soft, and have two paler "stripes" (shallow indented channels) impressed into their tops, dividing the top of the roll into three parts. Teleras are one of the easiest breads in the world to make, but making them ahead is the best method if you are planning to use them for hearty sandwiches—since they are so soft and fluffy when they first come out of the oven, it is best to wait a few hours or up to a day before slicing and filling them. At the very least, wait until they are completely cooled.

The only exception to the rule: teleras taste delicious fresh out of the oven with some queso fresco and drizzled honey in the middle—a nostalgic snack for me.

TELERAS

Mexican Sandwich Rolls   ○   Makes 6

1¼ cups warm
(not hot) water

2 tablespoons fresh
yeast, or 1 tablespoon
active dry yeast

4 cups all-purpose flour

2 tablespoons plus
1½ teaspoons sugar

1 tablespoon kosher salt

¼ cup rice bran oil or
canola oil

In a large bowl, whisk the water and yeast until incorporated. Add the flour and mix with your hands until smooth. Cover the bowl and set in a warm place to rise until doubled in size, about 1 hour.

In the clean bowl of a stand mixer fitted with a dough hook, combine the sugar, salt, and oil. Add the dough and mix on low speed until the mixture is smooth and elastic.

Line a baking sheet with parchment paper. Divide the dough into 6 equal balls (about 4 ounces each). Using the palm of your hand, press each ball into an oval shape. Using the long, thin handle of a wooden spoon, imprint two channels lengthwise into each piece, dividing the tops of each roll into three equal sections without cutting all the way through.

Transfer the pieces to the prepared baking sheet and cover loosely with plastic wrap. Let rest in a warm place until doubled in size, about 1 hour.

Preheat the oven to 375°F. Uncover the rolls and bake, rotating the pan halfway through baking, until golden brown, 12 to 14 minutes. Transfer to a wire rack and let cool completely before using or storing. Wrap in plastic wrap or store in a resealable plastic bag. Use within 3 to 4 days fresh, or freeze.

Cemita has two meanings: it is a big round sandwich from Puebla, Mexico, stacked high with fillings, usually prepared by street vendors. But the word also refers to the squishy sesame rolls on which cemitas are classically served. Lightly sweet, they are probably most similar to a brioche. But they are very easy to make.

CEMITAS

Sesame Sandwich Rolls   ○   Makes 6

1½ teaspoons anise seeds

1¼ cups warm (not hot) water

2 tablespoons fresh yeast, or 1 tablespoon active dry yeast

4 cups all-purpose flour, divided

¼ cup rice bran oil or canola oil

2 tablespoons plus 1½ teaspoons sugar

1 tablespoon kosher salt

1 egg

2 tablespoons toasted sesame seeds

Place the anise seeds and water in a blender and puree.

Place the yeast in a medium bowl and add the blender contents; whisk until the yeast dissolves. Add 2 cups of the flour and stir with a spatula until incorporated. Cover the bowl with plastic wrap and set in a warm place to rise until doubled in size, about 1 hour.

Line a baking sheet with parchment paper. In a larger bowl, mix the oil, sugar, and salt. Add the dough and the remaining 2 cups flour; mix with a spatula and eventually knead with your hands (alternatively, you can use a stand mixer fitted with a dough hook) until the flour is incorporated and the dough is smooth and elastic. Divide into 6 equal balls and transfer them to the prepared baking sheet. Using the palm of your hand, press them down a little to flatten slightly, then cover loosely with plastic wrap. Let sit in a warm place until doubled in size, about 1 hour.

Preheat the oven to 375°F. In a small bowl, beat the egg. Uncover the rolls and, using a pastry brush, brush the tops of the rolls with some of the egg and sprinkle with the sesame seeds. Bake, rotating the pan halfway through baking, until puffy and golden, 10 to 12 minutes. Transfer to a wire rack and let cool completely before using or storing. Wrap in plastic wrap or store in a resealable plastic bag. Use within 3 to 4 days fresh, or freeze.

In Mexico, *escabeche* refers to an array of different foods that have been preserved (pickled) in vinegar. Pickled red onions specifically are a little more common in the south of Mexico, where they are served with different regional antojitos, like *panuchos*—bean-filled, meat-topped tortillas. To play off the spiciness, we added habaneros to this recipe, which give the onions a hint of their flavor and heat.

ESCABECHE ROJO

Pickled Red Onions ○ Makes 3 to 4 cups

2 tablespoons olive oil

3 garlic cloves, halved

1 habanero chile, quartered

2 bay leaves

¾ teaspoon dried thyme

¾ teaspoon dried oregano

¾ teaspoon ground allspice

1½ teaspoons kosher salt

4 cups thinly sliced red onions (⅛ inch thick), from about 2 medium onions

¼ cup plus 2 tablespoons red wine vinegar

In a skillet over medium heat, heat the oil. Add the garlic, habanero, bay leaves, thyme, oregano, allspice, and salt and cook, stirring occasionally, until the garlic turns golden brown, about 2 minutes. Add the onions and cook, stirring occasionally, for 1 minute. Pour in the vinegar and stir well to deglaze the pan; cook for 1 minute.

Remove from the heat and transfer the onions and liquid to a large mason jar or other heatproof container; cover with plastic wrap and let cool to room temperature (about 4 hours). Cover with an airtight lid and store in the refrigerator. Will keep for several months.

In Mexico, we serve jalapeños alongside almost everything. The pickled version keeps forever and gives the added bonus of a pop of acidity, perfect for topping tacos or other antojitos. Along with a little crumbled queso fresco, they can work wonders atop a simple side of beans.

JALAPEÑOS CURTIDOS

Pickled Jalapeños ○ Makes 8 cups

2 tablespoons rice bran oil or canola oil

1 bay leaf

1 clove garlic

¾ teaspoon dried oregano

½ teaspoon freshly ground allspice

½ teaspoon dried thyme

½ teaspoon dried marjoram

2 tablespoons piloncillo or brown sugar

2 tablespoons kosher salt

1½ cups white onion, sliced 1 inch thick

1½ cups carrots, sliced ⅛ inch thick

4 cups jalapeños (from about 12), halved lengthwise, then sliced into ⅛-inch-thick half moons

½ cup apple cider vinegar

½ cup water

In a large pot, heat the oil until very hot. Add the bay leaf, garlic, oregano, allspice, thyme, marjoram, piloncillo, and salt. Cook, stirring occasionally, until the garlic turns golden brown, about 3 minutes. Add the onions and carrots and stir to incorporate. Add the jalapeños and cook, stirring occasionally, until some of the skins start to peel off, 3 to 5 minutes. Pour in the vinegar and water and let cook until at least half of the jalapeños have dulled in color and softened slightly, about 5 minutes.

Divide the vegetables between two quart-sized mason jars or similar-sized heatproof containers, then pour the remaining liquid on top. Cover the containers with plastic wrap and let sit until fully cooled. Refrigerate overnight before eating. Will keep for up to 1 month refrigerated.

Open the fridge of any Mexican home cook or chef, and you will find a jar or two of pickled vegetables. Traditionally, they are made with whatever vegetables are on hand, and the brine usually has a sweet-spicy quality from a combination of jalapeños and a little sugar. We call this style of chopped pickled vegetables *para tacos* because of their petite size—the idea is that you can spoon these pickles right on top of tacos, or eat little bites of them on the side. But they are delicious with any antojito.

CURTIDOS "PARA TACOS"

Pickled Vegetables　○　Makes about 4 cups

1½ cups carrots, halved lengthwise, then sliced into half moons

1½ cups jalapeños, halved lengthwise, then sliced into half moons

1½ cups small cauliflower florets (¾-inch pieces)

¼ white onion, thinly sliced

1 tablespoon plus 2 teaspoons kosher salt

1 cup white vinegar

1 tablespoon plus 1½ teaspoons sugar

1 bay leaf

2 cloves garlic

½ teaspoon dried marjoram

¾ teaspoon dried thyme

¾ teaspoon ground allspice

In a large bowl, combine the carrots, jalapeños, cauliflower, and onion; toss with the salt and let rest for 30 minutes.

In a medium pot, combine 1 cup water with the vinegar, sugar, bay leaf, garlic, marjoram, thyme, and allspice and bring to a boil.

Transfer the vegetables and salt to a 1-quart mason jar or comparable container. Pour the boiling vinegar mixture over the top and cover the jar with plastic wrap. Let cool slightly, then cover with a secure lid and let rest in the refrigerator for at least 8 hours before eating. Will keep for 2 to 4 weeks refrigerated.

Chipotle chiles actually come from fresh jalapeños that have been fully ripened, then smoked and dried. One of the most common ways you will see them in Mexican cooking is simmered and preserved in an *adobo*, a thick chile paste, in this case made from a mixture of more chipotles, tomatoes, and aromatics. You can use Chipotles Adobados as a hot sauce for meats such as carne asada, as an ingredient in a braising liquid or stew, or to add spice and smokiness to soups such as Caldo Tlalpeño (page 143).

CHIPOTLES ADOBADOS

Chipotles in Adobo Sauce ○ Makes 2 cups

2 cups dried chipotle chiles

¾ cup (6 ounces) diced canned tomatoes and their juices

½ carrot, peeled and finely chopped

2 tablespoons chopped white onion

1 clove garlic

2 tablespoons piloncillo or brown sugar

¼ teaspoon ground allspice

1 small bay leaf

¾ teaspoon dried marjoram

¾ teaspoon dried cumin

¼ teaspoon ground cinnamon

2 tablespoons apple cider vinegar

3 tablespoons olive oil

Salt

Using the tip of a paring knife, score the chiles with small holes all over. Transfer them to a medium pot and add enough water just to cover. Bring to a boil, then reduce to a simmer and let cook for 30 minutes. Set aside to cool.

Meanwhile, in a blender, combine the tomatoes, carrot, onion, garlic, piloncillo, allspice, bay leaf, marjoram, cumin, cinnamon, and vinegar; blend until smooth.

In a medium pot, heat the olive oil over medium-high heat. Once it's hot, pour in the blended salsa quickly and all at once (be careful, as the mixture may splash); bring to a boil, then reduce to a simmer and cook for 15 minutes.

Drain the chiles, discarding their soaking water, and add to the salsa; cook for an additional 10 minutes.

Let cool completely, then transfer to an airtight container. Will keep for a few weeks in the refrigerator.

Making mayonnaise from scratch takes just a few minutes and can be a fun project to do at home and feel proud of. We make ours with lime juice, but if necessary you can substitute lemon juice or a pale vinegar. It's up to you if you want to whisk your mayo by hand or use a blender, but just know that if you decide to go by hand, a good arm workout is coming your way.

MAYONNAISE

Makes about 1 cup

1 egg

1 tablespoon freshly squeezed lime juice

1 cup rice bran oil or canola oil

1 teaspoon kosher salt

In a mixing bowl or the bowl of a blender, whisk or blend together the egg and lime juice. Starting with a very small amount, slowly trickle in the oil while whisking vigorously or with the blender motor running. Continue drizzling the oil in as you continuously whisk or blend until the mixture is thickened and emulsified. Stir in the salt. Store refrigerated in an airtight container for up to 4 days.

Yet another way Mexicans use corn, hominy is made from dried corn kernels that are treated with lime, cal, or another alkaline ingredient to loosen their hulls as well as soften and puff up the kernels. In other words, it is *nixtamal* (see page 7), or the corn used to make masa. You can turn dried hominy into deep-fried corn nuts and toss with salt and Nopalito Spices (page 35), or prepare braised by following this recipe. The most common use for cooked hominy is in pozoles and ceviches.

MAIZ PARA POZOLE

Hominy   ○   Makes about 12 cups

4 cups dried white hominy (we prefer the Rancho Gordo brand)

1 tablespoon kosher salt

Preheat the oven to 350°F. Place the hominy in a large pot or Dutch oven and add enough water to cover by about 2 inches. Stir in the salt.

Cover the pot and transfer to the oven. Bake until the hominy is tender and doubled in volume, about 2 hours.

Remove and strain if using that day. If storing, let cool and then refrigerate the hominy in its liquid.

Chorizo is a pork sausage, very popular in Mexico, made by combining the ground meat with a long list of spices and ground chiles. Since at the restaurant we most often use chorizo removed from its casings, this is a recipe for the raw, loose meat, which can be sautéed and used in a variety of ways. We feature it in the Carne Asada (page 155), as well as the Potato Gorditas (page 113). But it is also delicious with eggs in the morning, stuffed inside chiles rellenos, or in a seafood stew containing clams or mussels.

This recipe makes a generous amount—enough to incorporate into several recipes—because chorizo freezes well.

CHORIZO OAXAQUEÑO

Makes about 6 cups (about 2½ pounds)

To prepare the adobo, heat a griddle or large skillet to medium heat. Add all of the chiles, working in batches if needed to fit them, and cook, flipping them every 10 seconds, until they blister and darken in places, 30 seconds to 1 minute. Remove from the heat, transfer the chiles to a heatproof bowl, and cover with boiling water; let sit 30 minutes.

Place the chiles in a blender and add a little of the soaking water as needed to help blend; puree until smooth. Set aside to cool completely.

Meanwhile, grind the pork and pork fat; if possible, first chill the parts of the meat grinder and the pork cubes and fat cubes in the freezer to get them as cold as possible. Remove everything just before grinding. Grind the meat and fat separately on the large setting, then mix them together.

In the bowl of a stand mixer, combine the chile puree with the remaining adobo ingredients (garlic, herbs, and spices) and stir well. Add the ground pork and fat, salt, and vinegar and mix well to distribute evenly. Cover the bowl and refrigerate overnight. Freeze the chorizo raw until ready to use, or use as desired, being sure to cook it fully before consuming.

Adobo

15 medium dried guajillo chiles, stemmed and seeded

3 medium dried ancho chiles, stemmed and seeded

7 medium dried puya chiles, stemmed and seeded

12 medium dried árbol chiles, stemmed and seeded

12 cloves garlic, chopped

3¾ teaspoons ground cumin

3¾ teaspoons dried oregano

2¼ teaspoons dried marjoram

2¼ teaspoons dried thyme

2¼ teaspoons Nopalito Spices (page 35) or 1⅛ teaspoons each chili powder and smoked hot paprika

¾ teaspoon ground cinnamon

¾ teaspoon freshly ground black pepper

¾ teaspoon ground allspice

¾ teaspoon ground coriander

¾ teaspoon ground nutmeg

¾ teaspoon ground ginger

½ teaspoon ground cloves

Meat and Additional Seasonings

1¾ pounds (28 ounces) cold boneless pork shoulder, cut into small (½-inch) cubes

¾ pound (12 ounces) cold pork fat, cut into small (½-inch) cubes

5 tablespoons kosher salt

1 cup apple cider vinegar

In Mexico, even the kids like spicy foods, so we grew up snacking on peanuts squeezed with a little lime juice and tossed with ground chiles. I still love spiced peanuts today—snacking on them, but also chopping them atop salads to add a little crunch and heat to the greens. The oven is probably the easiest way to toast the nuts, but you can also griddle them on a comal, which will give you a little more of a delicious charred flavor.

1 cup raw unsalted peanuts

2 tablespoons freshly squeezed lime juice (from about 1 large lime)

½ teaspoon kosher salt

¼ teaspoon Nopalito Spices (page 35) or ⅛ teaspoon each chili powder and smoked hot paprika

SPICED PEANUTS

Makes 1 cup

Preheat the oven to 350°F. Place the peanuts on a small baking sheet or ovenproof skillet and roast, stirring once, until toasted, about 6 minutes.

Meanwhile, in a medium bowl, stir together the lime juice, salt, and Nopalito spices until the salt is dissolved.

Add the roasted peanuts to the bowl with the lime mixture (this should create steam); toss as needed. Spread out on a plate and let rest until completely cooled and dry. (If there is any remaining liquid at this point, heat the peanuts for 5 minutes more, either on the baking sheet in the hot oven or in a dry skillet.)

RECOMMENDED TOOLS (AND SOME EXTRAS THAT ARE NICE TO HAVE)

Looking at the kitchen tools of old-world Mexico, you can easily see the strong connection between the food and the labor of love behind it. When I was growing up, not only was much of the local cooking done with manual tools, but the tools were handmade by craftspeople using natural materials like wood, stone, and mud. These rustic tools were and still are beautiful, but little by little they are being left behind by the new generations, who are incorporating store-bought products and electric kitchen appliances.

I realize it takes some effort to go out and buy—and to use—some of these more traditional tools, which is why most of the recipes in this book can be made using basic modern tools and appliances you might already have in your kitchen. But I hope you will find the beauty and utility in these rustic tools.

FOR EVERY DAY

MOLCAJETE ○ You have probably seen this classic round stone mortar and pestle used for serving guacamole at some restaurants. But it has many different uses in traditional Mexican cooking, where it was the go-to tool for crushing and grinding spices, making chile pastes, breaking down aromatics like garlic and onions, and preparing salsas (we still call these coarse-textured salsas "*salsas molcajetes*"). Molcajetes are said to season over time and use, much like cast-iron skillets or griddles. Maybe it's mental, or has something to do with the way the stone tears into the ingredients, helping to better release their flavors and oils, but ingredients ground up in a molcajete seem to taste more vibrant than those prepped in a blender, food processor, or electric spice grinder.

TORTILLA PRESS ○ If you plan to work with masa, which I highly recommend you do, you will need a tortilla press. They don't take up much space in the kitchen and are not too costly, and there is no substitute for pressing masa for thin homemade tortillas or masa bases for gorditas, panuchos, and empanadas. I prefer the wood

or metal models, or at least a heavier model—the light, flimsy ones will not work as well or turn out consistent shapes and thicknesses. To prevent sticking, don't forget to always line a tortilla press before using it: the classic way is to cut two big circles out of a plastic bag and place one underneath the ball of masa and another on top before clamping down. And remember: practice makes perfect.

COMAL ○ Although all of the recipes in this book can be made using skillets and Dutch ovens, we Mexicans are partial to using the *comal*—a wide, flat griddle. You will still see comals in many home kitchens and street stalls in Mexico, as well as in Mexican restaurants both there and in the United States. What's great about them is the ample space they offer for lining up many ingredients at once—you are not restricted to the confines of a 9-inch or 12-inch skillet, and you can move foods from hotter to colder zones instantly as needed. There is no rim on the edge of a comal to interfere with your flipping and turning of foods with a spatula, tongs, or your fingers. And a well-made, heavy comal also provides an even, steady transfer of heat. A final advantage: a comal that has been well-seasoned with use will allow you to char, sear, and cook foods with very little cooking fat, or sometimes no fat at all.

DEEP-FAT THERMOMETER ○ If you don't have a deep fryer at home, it is easy to rig one up with a high-sided pot and a deep-fat thermometer, which clips to the side of any high-sided pot. Temperature is the key to ensuring fried foods are cooked properly all the way through and don't come out greasy.

FOR EXTRA CREDIT

MOLINO DE MANO ○ Once again, it is no secret that I am a big supporter of making masa from scratch, and it is impossible to do so without a molino, or traditional corn grinder. At Nopalito we have an industrial-sized grinder that operates electrically, but the classic, manual home versions known as *molinos de manos* are petite,

easy to store, and easy to use. They function similarly to countertop pasta machines: you add the prepared nixtamal, making sure it is moist enough to slide through the molino easily, then crank the handle to break it down into a fine meal. I usually suggest running the nixtamal through a molino de mano twice to get it as finely ground and smooth as possible.

METATE ○ Some tasks of ultratraditional, old-school Mexican cooking are easier than others. Using a *metate* is more of a commitment for hard-core traditionalists—when I was growing up, every mom and abuelita in our village had one. The Mexican version of this tool is a large, shallow mortar or grinding slab, usually slightly concave in the center, and it comes with a large pestle often shaped like a rolling pin. Metates are most useful if you are grinding large amounts of an ingredient, like nixtamal for masa, or a larger number of chiles, spices, or seeds.

MOLINILLO ○ One of the most special items in the traditional Mexican kitchen is a *molinillo*, an ornately carved wooden tool used to foam up drinks, especially Mexican hot chocolate. To use a molinillo, you place the perforated round end into a mug or pot of liquid. Then, holding the stick between your palms, rapidly twirl it back and forth (as if you were trying to start a fire with two sticks). The motion infuses air into the drink, creating an aerated froth. If you don't have a molinillo you can use a whisk, but the effect is not quite the same.

CAZUELA ○ The word *cazuela* is used in Mexico as well as many parts of South America and Spain. It broadly refers to a style of wide, shallow earthenware pots and dishes, classically featuring two handles. In traditional Mexican cooking, cazuelas were used to cook nearly everything over fire—moles, beans, stews, and more. Nowadays, most are wide and flat, and they come in individual as well as larger sizes (which are more the Spanish style). We use them for baking and serving *queso flameado* (page 70), as well as some brunch and other dishes that get heated in the oven before serving.

Platillos Pequeños
(SMALL PLATES)

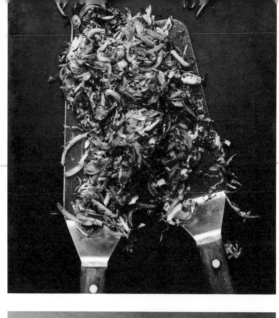

MOST OF THE CASUAL, EVERYDAY MEALS IN MEXICO ARE MADE UP OF *ANTOJITOS*, A WORD THAT MEANS "CRAVINGS."

This category of food encompasses small plates like quesadillas, tacos, gorditas, tamales, huaraches, and tostadas, to name just a few. Each town has at least a few kiosks where street vendors dish up hot antojitos all day, complete with an array of salsas, pickled vegetables, and other garnishes. These casual dishes are also made in every home kitchen, where families gobble them up one by one as quickly as they come off the comal. Whether you choose to eat one type of antojito or combine several kinds to make a meal, the idea is to snack on these small plates until you are satisfied.

Although there is much variety in fillings and toppings across the various states of Mexico, almost all of these small plates have a few things in common. For one, they feature masa in some form, as either a fresh tortilla, a crispy tostada shell, or a rich empanada pastry. Atop or inside these various forms of masa, you might find braised meats, seared fish, or certain types of vegetables depending on the time of year and the region. And almost always, small plates are garnished with a variety of colorful fresh garnishes like sliced white onion, shredded green cabbage, chopped fresh cilantro leaves, or tangy crema to provide contrast and brightness for each dish.

Just as the exact recipe varies from region to region and cook to cook, you should feel free to create your own, swapping the toppings and fillings in this section based on what is seasonally available or whatever you might be craving. Sometimes, the whole fun of antojitos is to taste as many different things as you can.

In western Mexico by the coast, local bars will serve this ceviche made with local fish for free—as long as you are paying for drinks. As far as ceviches go, this is a good one to serve in big batches at a party, or make a dinner out of by piling onto tostadas, because shrimp tends to be more affordable than other types of fish or shellfish.

Almost every ingredient here is traditional, including the grated carrots, which mix with the oniony, citrusy ceviche juice to lend a sweet flavor. It's a spicy dish, so feel free to substitute jalapeños if serranos have too much heat for you.

CEVICHE NAYARITA DE CAMARÓN

Shrimp Ceviche from Nayarit　◦　Serves 6

1 pound fresh shrimp, preferably the white Gulf variety, peeled, cleaned, and finely chopped

1 cup freshly squeezed lime juice (from 6 to 8 limes), plus more as needed

¼ red onion, finely chopped

1¾ teaspoons kosher salt, plus more as needed

½ cup grated carrots, grated on the large holes of a box grater

½ cup finely diced cucumber, peeled if desired

1 to 3 serrano chiles, finely chopped

¼ cup chopped fresh cilantro leaves

2 tablespoons sliced green onions

Extra-virgin olive oil, for drizzling

Tortilla chips or salted crackers, for serving

In a large bowl, combine the shrimp, lime juice, red onions, and salt. Let sit for 10 minutes, stirring occasionally. Add the carrots, cucumber, chiles, cilantro, and green onions and stir to combine. Taste and adjust the lime juice and salt as needed. Drizzle lightly with olive oil and serve immediately with the chips.

This makes the best snack with a six-pack of Mexican beer or some ice-cold tequila and a mountain of chips. Usually making a recipe *à la Mexicana* means using tomatoes, onions, and jalapeños (the colors of the Mexican flag), which is why this dish is best served when fresh tomatoes are coming into season but Dungeness crab is still kicking around. Roma tomatoes are the classic choice in Mexico, but I like the cherry variety because they hold their shape and aren't as soupy when chopped.

Crab is popular in Mexican ceviches and adds a nice soft consistency when mixed with the shrimp, but if it is too hard to find or too time-consuming to pluck from the shells, or you simply prefer all shrimp, feel free to omit the crab and up the quantity of shrimp by 1 cup. And if you have a hankering for extra spice, top the finished dish with thinly sliced serrano chiles, or a spicy Pequin Hot Sauce (page 234).

CEVICHE DE CAMARÓN Y CANGREJO À LA MEXICANA

Shrimp and Crab Ceviche with Tomatoes, Onions, and Jalapeños ○ Serves 6 to 8

1 cup plus 2 tablespoons freshly squeezed lime juice (from about 8 limes), or more as needed

Salt

2 cups finely chopped cleaned shrimp (from about 1½ pounds), preferably the white Gulf variety

½ small white onion, finely diced

1 cup chilled Dungeness crab meat (from about 1 large crab)

2 jalapeños, finely chopped

½ bunch fresh cilantro leaves, chopped

2 cups small cherry tomatoes, halved, or chopped heirloom tomatoes

Tortilla chips or salted crackers, for serving

Set a small pot of water on the stove and stir in 2 tablespoons lime juice; season generously with salt, so it tastes like the ocean, and bring to a boil. Add the shrimp and cook until just pink and opaque, 30 seconds to 1 minute. Strain and spread the shrimp pieces out in a single layer to dry and cool completely; chill. (At this point you can refrigerate the shrimp until ready to use, up to 2 days.)

In a medium serving bowl, combine the onion and the remaining 1 cup lime juice; let rest for 5 minutes, then add the shrimp and crab meat, jalapeños, and cilantro. Stir in the tomatoes just before serving. Taste and adjust the salt and lime juice as needed. Serve with the chips.

HOW TO PREPARE DUNGENESS CRAB

If you can't find par-cooked crab in stores, you can boil live crab yourself in less then 20 minutes. Be sure to allow time for the crab to cool completely. After that, you can refrigerate cooked crab up to 2 days in advance.

Bring a large pot of water to a boil and add enough salt so the water tastes like the ocean. Add the crab(s) and boil until the color has brightened and the meat is just cooked through, about 16 minutes for a medium crab. Remove and transfer to a sheet pan or strainer to cool completely. Crack the crabs into pieces, splitting the bodies in half, then breaking open all the joints with the help of a crab cracker or kitchen shears. Rinse away any colored material on the inside with cold running water if desired, then pick out all the meat. Cover and refrigerate until ready to use.

This is a robust red ceviche you can make any time of year because the ingredients are always accessible. Feel free to prepare the individual ingredients in advance (except the avocado, which needs to be cut at the last moment to prevent it from browning as it sits). But since the fish is meant to be served completely raw, wait until the last minute to stir it all together.

2 medium dried árbol chiles, stemmed and seeded

3 dried guajillo chiles, stemmed and seeded

2 cups diced skinless halibut fillet

Salt

½ cup freshly squeezed lime juice (from 3 to 4 limes), plus more as needed

¼ cup thinly sliced red onion

1 small jalapeño, finely chopped

2 tablespoons chopped fresh cilantro

⅓ cup diced firm-ripe avocado

Tortilla chips, tortillas, or salted crackers, for serving

CEVICHE DE PESCADO CON CHILE GUAJILLO

Halibut Ceviche with Red Chiles ○ Serves 4 to 6

Place the árbol and guajillo chiles in a medium heatproof bowl and add enough boiling water to cover; let sit until the chiles are softened, about 20 minutes. Remove the chiles (reserve the soaking water) and transfer them to a blender or molcajete; puree to form a smooth paste, adding some of the soaking water as needed to blend.

Transfer the chile mixture to a medium bowl. When ready to serve, season the halibut with salt and stir it into the chile mixture along with the lime juice and red onions. Let rest for 5 minutes, then stir in the jalapeño and cilantro.

Transfer the ceviche to a serving bowl and top with the avocado. Serve immediately with the chips.

This was the first ceviche we served at Nopalito, and it has stuck around ever since. It was inspired by a street-food vendor in northern coastal Mexico, where the cook finely diced tomatillos to make a chunky texture similar to a pico de gallo. Our twist is to blend the tomatillos a little to make the whole dish greener but still leave it chunky enough that you can see the tomatillo pieces.

In Mexico there is a tradition called *campechana* of blending two kinds of fish—one less expensive than the other—in a ceviche or chilled cocktail-style preparation to help stretch the dish so you can feed more people for less. This is one reason we use calamari (squid) along with fresh local cod. If you can't find calamari fresh or you prefer all cod, you can omit the calamari or substitute something similar, like octopus. Use the three jalapeños if you want a more fiery ceviche.

CEVICHE VERDE DE PESCADO Y CALAMARI

Green Ceviche with White Fish and Calamari   ○   Serves 6 to 8

1½ pounds fresh, cleaned calamari, tentacles trimmed into bite-sized pieces, tubes cut into 1-inch squares

Salt

12 medium tomatillos (about 2 pounds), husked, rinsed, dried, and halved

Leaves from 1 large bunch cilantro (about 2½ cups)

2 to 3 jalapeños, finely chopped

3 cloves garlic, coarsely chopped

2 cups diced, skinned ling cod (rock cod) or other meaty white fish

1 cup freshly squeezed lime juice (from about 8 limes)

Tortilla chips or salted crackers, for serving

Bring a medium pot of water to a boil. Meanwhile, set a medium bowl of ice water next to the stove. Season both the ice water and the pot of water generously with salt (both should taste as salty as the ocean). Once the water is boiling, add the calamari and let cook until firmed up slightly, 1½ to 2 minutes. Using a slotted spoon, quickly transfer the calamari to the ice water to cool. Remove when cold and drain well.

In a blender, combine the tomatillos, cilantro, jalapeños, garlic, and a pinch or two of salt; pulse until just chunky. Drain the mixture over a medium bowl and discard about two-thirds of the liquid (you should have a little less than 1 cup remaining). In a medium serving bowl, combine the remaining liquid with the chunky tomatillo mixture. (The recipe can be prepared to this point up to a day in advance; refrigerate the components separately.)

When ready to serve, in a separate medium bowl, combine the calamari, cod, and lime juice and let sit, stirring occasionally, for 5 minutes. Stir the fish mixture into the tomatillo mixture, then taste and adjust the amount of salt and lime juice. Serve immediately with the chips.

How to Clean Whole Calamari

Slice the whole calamari in half lengthwise and scrape out all the insides, including any of the clear film that clings to the interior. Trim away the eyes and ink sac and remove any hard pieces of cartilage. Separate the tentacles from the tube.

When we were growing up in Mexico, fried chile-and-lime-spiced peanuts were the snack we would eat while hanging around, watching movies, or waiting for dinner. Since it is difficult to find organic peanuts in California (and they can be expensive), we tried the recipe with fried dried chickpeas instead. It works perfectly, and the crunchy, salty little chickpeas are addictive.

While you can use store-bought chili powders, making your own is easy and the result is so much more flavorful. Feel free to play with the amount and type, such as upping the ratio of guajillos, which are less spicy than the chiles de árbol.

This recipe will seem like it makes a ton of chickpeas while you are cooking, but don't worry: the chickpeas will shrink down significantly when they fry.

4 cups dried chickpeas

5 tablespoons kosher salt, divided

2 quarts rice bran oil or canola oil

2 tablespoons Nopalito Spices (page 35) or store-bought Mexican chili powder

GARBANZOS CON CHILE

Fried Chickpeas with Chili Powder ○ Makes 4 cups

Preheat the oven to 350°F. Add the chickpeas to a large ovenproof pot, then fill with water. Add 3 tablespoons of the salt, cover the pot, transfer to the oven, and bake for 2 hours. Remove and drain completely in a colander. Let the chickpeas cool.

Set a medium-large heatproof bowl next to the stove. Add the oil to a large, deep-sided skillet or pot, and heat until it registers 350°F on a deep-fat thermometer. Add the chickpeas and let cook until golden-brown and crunchy, about 15 minutes.

Using a slotted spoon or spider skimmer, remove the chickpeas and transfer them to the bowl. While they're still hot, mix them with the chili powder and the remaining 3 tablespoons salt. Let cool completely and serve. Will keep for 7 to 10 days stored in an airtight container.

It's funny that when you go to a Mexican restaurant in America, the first thing you can expect is to get free chips and salsa (this is not the tradition in Mexico). This recipe is meant to play around with that idea—the word *totopos* means "chips" in Spanish, and instead of serving them with the standard dip, we bake the chips, then toss them in warm salsa, similar to the way chicken wings are made.

You can prepare the salsa in advance and heat it up when it's time for tossing with the chips. It has a lot of heat and a good amount of acidity, thanks to the tomatillo and vinegar. The crema, drizzled on at the end or served on the side, is there to help to cool the spice and contrast with the acidity. A squeeze bottle is a good way to drizzle on the perfect amount.

2 cups Salsa de Árbol
(page 233)

16 ounces homemade salted corn tortilla chips (see page 66) or thick, hearty store-bought chips

1 cup grated Cotija cheese

½ cup finely diced white onion

½ cup fresh cilantro leaves, finely chopped

1 cup Crema (page 35) or sour cream

Lime wedges, for serving

TOTOPOS CON CHILE

Baked Tortilla Chips Tossed with Spicy Salsa de Árbol   ○   Serves 8

Be sure your salsa de árbol is prepared in advance and is still hot, or reheat on the stove. Preheat the oven to 450°F. Spread the chips on a baking sheet and bake until warmed through, about 2 minutes.

Transfer the chips from the oven to a large mixing bowl. Add the salsa and toss the chips with the hot salsa until they are completely covered. Transfer to a serving plate, then garnish the chips with the cheese, onion, and cilantro. Serve with the crema and lime wedges.

HOW TO FRY
YOUR OWN
TORTILLA CHIPS

Your best bet is to start with homemade soft corn tortillas between one and four days old. The extra time dries them out slightly, preventing them from turning out too greasy when fried. In a pinch, you can also use store-bought soft corn tortillas—no need to age these for a day, as they are naturally drier than homemade tortillas.

A deep fryer makes this process easier, but you can also fry chips on the stove top. Here's how to do either:

Cut some soft corn tortillas into the size and shape of chips you want. (If making strips to garnish salads or other meals—like Ensalada de Lechuga, page 78—cut the tortillas into thin ribbons.)

Line a baking sheet with paper towels. Fill a deep fryer with rice bran oil or canola oil and heat to 350°F; alternatively, fill a large pot with enough rice bran or canola oil to reach 2 inches up the sides of the pan, and heat until it registers 350°F on a deep-fat thermometer. Add as many chips as can fit without overcrowding and let cook, rotating and turning the chips occasionally with a spoon, until deep golden and completely hard and crunchy, 5 to 8 minutes (try not to overcook them, as this can make them greasy as well).

Remove with a slotted spoon or spider and transfer to the paper towels to drain. Season with salt while they're still hot.

To store, let the chips cool down completely, then store in a resealable bag at room temperature up to 4 days.

One of the things that makes our guacamole recipe special is the quality of the ingredients that go into it. We strive to find the very best, and usually that means local California avocados that are well-ripened and have the creamiest flesh (Hass is typically a good bet). If you do end up with avocados that are bland, try adding a little extra-virgin olive oil to boost their taste and creaminess.

Ample tartness and seasoning are our other secrets to a well-balanced guacamole. Since some limes can be sweeter or less acidic than others, make sure to add enough lime juice to give a burst of freshness and acidity to cut through the fatty avocados. In Mexico, some cooks use tomatoes or pico de gallo to the same end, but since they are not available year-round, we use fresh tomatillos. Finally, always season guacamole generously with salt.

GUACAMOLE

Makes about 5 cups ○ Serves 10 to 12

¼ large white onion, diced

2 tablespoons sliced green onion

2 tablespoons freshly squeezed lime juice (from 1 to 2 limes), plus more as needed

5 very ripe avocados, pitted and peeled

1 jalapeño, finely chopped (optional)

2 tablespoons chopped cilantro leaves

2 small-to-medium tomatillos, finely chopped

1 teaspoon kosher salt, plus more as needed

1 tablespoon extra-virgin olive oil (optional)

Salted corn tortilla chips, for serving

In a small bowl, combine the white onion, green onion, and lime juice; let sit for 5 minutes.

In a medium bowl, smash the avocados with a wooden spoon or a fork, leaving the mixture a little chunky. Add the onion mixture and the jalapeño (if using), the cilantro, and the tomatillos, and season with the salt; stir well to combine. Taste and adjust the lime juice and salt. Stir in the olive oil only if needed for creaminess and flavor. Serve immediately with the chips.

How to Select the Perfect Avocado

When I feel an avocado, I'm looking for signs that the flesh will be soft—but not too soft—all the way through to the pit. This will ensure the best creaminess and color for guacamole. From the outside, the fruit should feel slightly spongy but not smushy when lightly squeezed with all five of your fingertips. If some fingertips feel more resistance than others, the avocado may need a little more time to soften. Let it sit out at room temperature to ripen.

This delicious dish of molten cheese and crumbled, spiced chorizo is loved all over Mexico, but my favorite versions are in the southern part of the country, where cooks often add tender cactus leaves, or *nopales*. (Outside of Mexico you can usually find cactus at Mexican markets or online.) Once you have all the ingredients prepared and layered, it takes just 10 minutes in the oven.

A *cazuela* is a Spanish-style ovenproof dish; you can use any comparable casserole dish or cast-iron pot. Queso flameado is best eaten hot, so be sure to get it onto the table just as soon as it is out of the oven.

QUESO FLAMEADO CON CHORIZO Y NOPALES

Hot Oaxacan and Jack Cheese Dip with Chorizo and Cactus   ○   Serves 4

2 small nopales, spines trimmed away

Salt

2 teaspoons rice bran oil or canola oil

6 ounces (¾ cup) Chorizo Oaxaqueño (page 44) or crumbled store-bought Mexican chorizo (discard the casings)

1 cup shredded Jack cheese

⅔ cup shredded Oaxacan cheese (see page 27)

Chopped cilantro leaves

Tortilla chips or warm soft corn tortillas, for serving

Rinse the cactus leaves with cold water and pat them dry; season on both sides with salt. Preheat a skillet big enough to contain both cactus leaves over high heat (if they won't both fit, work in batches or in two separate skillets). Add the cactus leaves and cook, flipping them every 3 to 4 minutes, until well seared on both sides, about 15 minutes total. Transfer to a cutting board and let rest until cool enough to handle, then slice into thin, bite-sized strips.

Preheat the oven to 375°F. In a medium skillet, heat the oil over medium-high heat. Add the chorizo and cook, breaking up the meat into small pieces with a wooden spoon or spatula, until browned and cooked through, 6 to 8 minutes. Drain off any excess fat that pools in the bottom of the pan.

In a 16-ounce (6-inch) cazuela or other ovenproof baking dish, layer half of the Jack cheese evenly on the bottom. Top with a layer of the chorizo, then one-quarter of the Oaxacan cheese, the cactus strips, and the rest of the Jack and Oaxacan cheeses mixed together.

Set the dish on a baking sheet and bake until the cheese is completely melted and bubbling around the edges, about 10 minutes. Remove and garnish with cilantro leaves. Serve immediately with chips or tortillas for dipping.

Tropical fruit doused in chili powder and lime is a classic street food in Mexico. At the markets and food kiosks all over town, vendors sell sliced fruit in little plastic bags and pass out toppings that you can sprinkle on yourself. Fruit is also commonly paired with spicy salsas in Mexico, so we decided to combine all of these into one juicy salad. The queso fresco adds a touch of saltiness and creaminess, and the vinegar in the salsa helps cut some of the spice.

If you are in more of a savory mood, or melons are out of season, you can do this salad with light-flavored vegetables, like cucumbers, jicama, carrots, or a mix of citrus fruits.

ENSALADA DE FRUTAS

Fruit Salad with Chile and Lime   ○   Serves 4

¼ cup freshly squeezed lime juice (from 2 to 3 limes)

½ cup freshly squeezed orange juice (from 1 to 2 oranges)

1 teaspoon kosher salt

2 cups bite-sized watermelon cubes

4 cups bite-sized diced mixed melons or other tropical fruits of your choice, such as cantaloupe or pineapple

½ cup crumbled queso fresco

1 teaspoon Nopalito Spices (page 35)

1 tablespoon Salsa "Bufalo" (page 231)

In a large bowl, combine the lime juice, orange juice, and salt; whisk to dissolve the salt. Add the fruit and toss to coat in the citrus juice.

Transfer the fruit and all of the juices to a serving plate or bowl. Garnish with the queso fresco, Nopalito spices, and salsa.

Cactus grows just about everywhere in Mexico, so of course it only made sense for it to end up on our tables. As kids we would cut down the tender cactus leaves, or *nopales*, from our yards, trim away the spines, and eat them raw with salt as a snack. You can see nopales used in many Mexican recipes, from salsas to pico de gallos, scrambled with eggs for breakfast, used in stews and salads, and more.

The smaller the leaves, the more tender they will be. Salting them in advance will remove some of their natural sliminess.

ENSALADA DE NOPALES

Cactus Leaf Salad ○ Serves 4

3 medium nopales, spines trimmed away

¼ cup kosher salt, plus more as needed

12 slices red onion (from about ½ large onion)

¼ cup freshly squeezed lime juice (from 2 to 3 limes), divided

2 medium ripe tomatoes

1 avocado

¼ cup grated Cotija or ricotta salata cheese

1 tablespoon chopped fresh cilantro

Rinse the nopales and pat dry. Slice crosswise into ¼-inch strips and transfer to a colander set in the sink. Toss with ¼ cup kosher salt, then let macerate for about 30 minutes. Rinse the nopales under cold running water until most of the salt has been removed (this step will help minimize the sliminess of the cactus); drain well.

Meanwhile, in a large nonreactive skillet over medium heat, sauté the onions with 1 tablespoon of the lime juice and a pinch of salt, stirring occasionally, until the onions begin to turn pink, 2 to 3 minutes. Transfer to a small bowl, cover with plastic wrap, and let rest until cool.

When ready to serve, cut the tomatoes and avocado into ¼-inch cubes. In a serving bowl, gently toss the nopales, onions, tomatoes, avocados, and the remaining 3 tablespoons lime juice. Add salt to taste.

Divide the salad equally among four plates or arrange on a medium platter. Top with the cheese and cilantro.

Purslane is a succulent that happens to thrive in Northern California *and* in Mexico, among many other places in the world. Its plump little leaves are reminiscent of the texture of *nopales*, or cactus leaves. If you can't find purslane, you can substitute watercress in this dish. Either goes well with the dressing, a tart and tangy vinaigrette thickened with toasted pepitas (pumpkin seeds).

Make sure the toasted pepitas are fully cooled before you blend or process them, to avoid ending up with pepita butter. And remember to cut the cucumbers on the thicker side so they don't break down too much in the lime juice.

ENSALADA DE PEPINOS Y VERDOLAGAS

Cucumber and Purslane Salad   o   Serves 4

½ cup pepitas

½ cup freshly squeezed lemon juice (from 2 to 3 lemons)

¼ cup apple cider vinegar

1 cup extra-virgin olive oil

1 cup rice bran oil or canola oil

Salt

4 cups cucumber, halved lengthwise and sliced into thick half-moons

¼ cup freshly squeezed lime juice (from 2 to 3 limes)

4 cups cleaned purslane or watercress

1 avocado, pitted, peeled, and diced

1 cup crumbled queso fresco, for garnish

To make the dressing, preheat the oven to 350°F. Place the pepitas on a small baking sheet and roast until browned in places and aromatic, about 10 minutes. Remove and let cool completely.

Place half of the fully cooled pepitas in a food processor and grind into a coarse powder. Add the lemon juice and vinegar and mix thoroughly. With the motor running, slowly stream in both oils until the dressing is completely emulsified. Season with salt to taste.

Place the cucumber and lime juice in a large serving bowl and let marinate 5 minutes. Stir to distribute the lime juice, then add the purslane, avocado, and dressing to taste and toss gently to combine. Garnish with the queso fresco and the remaining ¼ cup of the toasted pepitas.

Salads in Mexico are usually made with simple, rustic ingredients such as cabbages, tomato wedges, or fruit, so this lettuce-based salad has more of a California influence than Mexican. If you can't find crisp Little Gem lettuces locally, you can substitute baby romaine.

To bring some Mexican flavors, we add jalapeños to this salad dressing. We smoke them first, which not only adds a unique flavor and complexity but also tempers the heat of the peppers. It is actually easy to do at home, even if you don't have a smoker (instructions follow). But if you would rather skip this step, follow the directions in the recipe for boiling the jalapeños; this similarly helps tame their heat.

Speaking of shortcuts, you can also swap in store-bought spiced peanuts, rather than making your own, though this recipe makes a little extra for snacking on.

ENSALADA DE LECHUGA CON MANZANA

Little Gem Salad with Apples and Jalapeño Vinaigrette　◦　Serves 4 to 6

¼ red onion, thinly sliced

1 small jalapeño, smoked if desired

¼ cup freshly squeezed lime juice (from 2 to 3 limes), divided

¼ teaspoon kosher salt, plus more for seasoning

Rice bran oil or canola oil, for deep-frying

2 soft corn tortillas (if using homemade, use 1-day-old), sliced into ¼-inch strips

¼ cup apple cider vinegar

½ cup extra-virgin olive oil

½ cup rice bran oil or canola oil

8 cups Little Gem lettuces

1 firm-ripe apple (Granny Smith or another tart variety), thinly sliced

6 radishes, very thinly sliced

1 avocado, pitted, peeled, and diced

½ cup Spiced Peanuts (page 45) or a spicy store-bought version

Shaved ricotta salata cheese, for garnish

Bring a small pot of water to a boil. Place the red onions in a small heatproof bowl and ladle some boiling water over to cover; let sit 5 minutes. Meanwhile, if you did not smoke the jalapeño, add it to the boiling water; boil until the chile is slightly softened and darkened, 8 to 10 minutes. Remove and let cool.

Drain the red onions and add 2 tablespoons of the lime juice and the ¼ teaspoon salt to the bowl; let sit so the onions pickle slightly, about 40 minutes. The onions should look pink at this point.

Set a paper towel–lined plate next to the stove. Use a deep fryer, or add enough of the oil to a medium pot so it comes 1 to 2 inches up the sides of the pan. Heat the oil until it registers 350°F on a deep-fat thermometer, then add the tortilla strips, working in batches if necessary to make sure they are completely submerged. Fry, turning occasionally, until very crispy, 5 to 8 minutes. Remove using a slotted spoon or spider and transfer to the prepared plate; season with salt while still warm.

To make the vinaigrette, transfer the jalapeño to a blender and add the vinegar and the remaining 2 tablespoons lime juice; blend until smooth. With the motor running, stream in the oils until emulsified; season with salt to taste.

In a large serving bowl, combine the lettuces, apple, and avocado; season with salt to taste and toss with ¼ cup plus 2 tablespoons of the vinaigrette (or more to taste). Garnish with the spiced peanuts and ricotta salata, the pickled onions, and the fried tortilla strips.

How to Smoke Jalapeños on the Stove Top (If You Don't Have a Smoker)

Soak a handful of wood chips in water for 30 minutes, then set them in a medium pot. Ignite the wood using a lighter until smoking. Place a metal vegetable steamer insert atop the pile, add a few jalapeños, and partially cover the pot. The chiles are done when the smoke stops rising.

Whether in the south of Mexico, where it is served boiled, or the north, where it is served charred, *esquite tostado* is ubiquitous among street vendors, who garnish it with mayonnaise, ground chile, and a wedge of lime for squeezing. We use crema or sour cream in place of mayonnaise—they have more acidity and tang than mayo and give a better contrast to the sweet corn.

For best results, serve this dish in summer, when corn is in season and the kernels are abundantly sweet and not too starchy.

ESQUITE TOSTADO CON CREMA Y QUESO

Toasted Corn with Crema, Ground Chile, and Queso Fresco   ○   Serves 4

Kernels cut from 3 ears fresh corn (about 4 cups)

2 tablespoons freshly squeezed lime juice (from 1 to 2 limes), plus 4 lime wedges, for serving

1 teaspoon kosher salt, plus more to taste

½ cup Crema (page 35) or sour cream

½ cup crumbled queso fresco

1 tablespoon Nopalito Spices (page 35) or 1½ teaspoons each ground chili powder and smoked paprika

¼ cup Pico de Gallo (recipe follows)

In a large skillet or griddle over high heat, cook the corn kernels, stirring occasionally, until lightly charred in places, about 5 minutes (be careful, as the corn may start "jumping"; lower the heat as needed). Stir in the lime juice and salt. Taste and adjust the seasoning and acidity as needed.

Divide the corn kernels among four individual bowls or place in one large serving bowl and top with the crema, queso fresco, Nopalito spices, and pico de gallo. Serve with lime wedges, and stir the toppings into the corn just before eating.

Pico de Gallo

½ small red onion, finely diced

2 tablespoons freshly squeezed lime juice (from 1 to 2 limes)

Salt

3 red tomatoes, finely diced

2 tablespoons chopped cilantro leaves

2 jalapeños, diced

½ bunch scallions, thinly sliced

Pico de Gallo

Makes about 1½ cups

In a medium bowl, stir together the red onion, lime juice, and a pinch of salt; let sit 5 minutes. Add the tomatoes, cilantro, jalapeños, and scallions. Taste and adjust the seasoning as needed.

Next to cheese, vegetables are the most popular filling in authentic Mexican quesadillas. Brussels sprouts, when slowly roasted and caramelized, develop a sweet earthiness that goes well with salty cheese. We shred and sauté the sprouts with homemade chile oil, so the leaves absorb the spice and flavor of the peppers.

Peanuts are often added to make salsa for the regional quesadillas of Veracruz. Here I've substituted sunflower seeds, which have a more subtle nutty flavor that goes great with the Brussels sprouts.

You can make the chile oil days or even weeks before you get started on the rest of the quesadilla. Use the extra oil with anything—drizzled on roasted vegetables, stirred into soups, or with fried eggs.

Cascabel Chile Oil

6 dried cascabel chiles, stemmed and seeded

1 dried guajillo chile, stemmed and seeded

1½ cups rice bran oil or canola oil

1 small clove garlic

Quesadillas

¼ cup rice bran oil or canola oil, plus more as needed

2 cups thinly sliced white onions

4 cups cored, thinly sliced Brussels sprouts (about 1 pound)

Kosher salt

4 homemade soft corn tortillas (see page 16) or 8 store-bought soft corn tortillas

1½ cups (12 ounces) shredded Oaxacan cheese or Jack cheese

For serving

Crumbled queso fresco

Fresh cilantro leaves

Salsa Macha (page 218; optional)

QUESADILLAS CON REPOLLO DE BRUSELAS

Quesadillas with Brussels Sprouts and Cascabel Chile Oil   ○   Serves 4

To make the chile oil, preheat the oven to 350°F. Place the cascabel and guajillo chiles on a baking sheet and roast until the guajillos turn dark red, about 5 minutes; remove, but do not turn off the oven.

Meanwhile, bring a small pot of water to a boil. Transfer the chiles to a medium heatproof bowl and cover with boiling water; let sit until the chiles are soft, about 20 minutes.

Drain the chiles and place them in a blender along with the 1½ cups oil and the garlic; blend until the oil becomes clear and red. Once it is fully cooled, the cascabel oil can be stored in an airtight container until ready to use.

To make the filling, in a large skillet, heat the ¼ cup oil over high heat. Add the onions and lower the heat to medium-high; cook, stirring occasionally, until softened and lightly browned in places, 5 to 6 minutes. Add the Brussels sprouts and season with salt; let cook, stirring occasionally, until the size of the leaves is reduced by half and their edges are beginning to brown, 5 to 7 minutes. Drizzle with 2 to 4 tablespoons of the chile oil to taste, and season with more salt as needed.

Preheat a large skillet or griddle to medium-high heat. Add all of the homemade or half of the store-bought tortillas, working in batches as needed to fit. Sprinkle the shredded cheese over one side of the homemade tortillas or across the full diameter of the store-bought ones. Quickly divide the Brussels sprouts mixture over the top (about ⅓ cup per quesadilla). Fold the homemade tortillas in half to cover; top store-bought tortillas with another whole tortilla to cover. Cook, flipping the quesadilla 1 to 2 times with a spatula, until the cheese is fully melted, 5 to 7 minutes total. Repeat with the remaining quesadillas as needed.

Transfer the quesadillas to four plates and garnish with the queso fresco and cilantro. Serve with the salsa macha if using.

Whereas tacos are often filled with richer foods like braised, grilled, or seared meats, quesadillas in Mexico are usually packed with seasonal vegetables. Although asparagus is not really a traditional Mexican ingredient, we feature it at Nopalito whenever sweet, tender asparagus is available in the spring. Made with a homemade corn tortilla and melted Oaxacan cheese, this quesadilla has plenty of authentic traits.

Since almost everything we eat in Mexico comes with a salsa, hot sauce, or other spicy accompaniment, we like to serve a fresh, medium-heat salsa with these.

¼ cup rice bran oil or canola oil, plus 1 teaspoon

2 cups thinly sliced white onions

4 cloves garlic

1 to 2 medium jalapeños, stemmed and finely chopped

Salt

1 large bunch asparagus spears, woody ends trimmed away, remainder sliced into thin coins (4 cups)

4 homemade soft corn tortillas (see page 16) or 8 store-bought soft corn tortillas

1½ cups (12 ounces) shredded Oaxacan cheese or Jack cheese

For serving

Crumbled queso fresco

Fresh cilantro leaves

Salsa Cilantro (page 218)

QUESADILLAS DE ESPARAGOS CON SALSA DE CILANTRO

Asparagus Quesadillas with Salsa Cilantro ○ Serves 4

To make the filling, in a medium skillet, heat the oil over medium-high heat. Add the onions, garlic, and jalapeños and season with salt. Cook, stirring occasionally, until the onions are translucent, 3 to 4 minutes. Stir in the asparagus, then turn off the heat and let cool slightly.

Preheat a griddle or large skillet over medium heat and drizzle the pan with about 1 teaspoon of oil. Add all of the homemade or 4 of the store-bought tortillas, working in batches as needed to fit. If using homemade, distribute a scant ⅓ cup cheese over half of each, then divide the asparagus mixture evenly, placing it over the cheese; fold the tortillas in half to cover the filling. If using store-bought tortillas, spread a layer of cheese (about 3 tablespoons) over the top of one whole tortilla, top with the asparagus and about 2 tablespoons more of the cheese, then top with a second whole tortilla. Cook, flipping the quesadillas once or twice, until the cheese is fully melted, 6 to 8 minutes total. Repeat with the remaining quesadillas as needed.

Transfer the quesadillas to four plates and garnish with the queso fresco and fresh cilantro. Serve with the cilantro salsa.

If you've never heard of a crunchy quesadilla, you are in for a treat. This style of quesadilla is griddled using more oil so that the tortilla actually gets crispy—similar to a crunchy taco shell—while the filling cooks inside. It is a style more typical of northern Mexico, and this version has a mixture of tender pork meat and crispy fried pork rinds, a play on traditional carnitas. Much of the dish's flavor comes from mixing both the shredded meat and the masa with dried chile–based salsas. But if you prefer a bit less work, you can use classic corn tortillas.

Though I've seen chicharrónes in the United States that are so light and airy they melt in your mouth, ours are heartier and have good crunch, and each mouthful lasts longer. Try topping any leftover chicharrónes with queso fresco and hot sauce—a Mexican snack we call *botanas*.

QUESADILLAS ROJAS CON CHICHARRÓNES

Crispy Red Quesadillas with Braised Red Pork and Pork Rinds   ○   Makes 4

Quesadillas

1 pound boneless pork shoulder

Salt

½ cup Salsa Para Quesadillas (recipe follows), plus more for serving

4 homemade soft ancho-corn tortillas (see page 16) or 8 store-bought corn tortillas

Salt

1½ cups (12 ounces) shredded Oaxacan cheese or Jack cheese

¼ cup rice bran oil or canola oil

For serving

Chicharrónes (recipe follows; optional)

Crumbled queso fresco

Fresh cilantro leaves

Finely chopped white onion

CONTINUED

Place the pork shoulder in a medium pot and fill with water to cover; season the water generously with salt. Bring to a boil, then reduce to a steady simmer and let cook until the meat is tender, about 2 hours. Drain, then shred the meat and mix with the ½ cup salsa.

Preheat a griddle or large skillet over medium heat, and wipe it with a thin layer of oil. Working in batches as needed for fit, cook the tortillas, flipping every 3 minutes, until puffed, about 9 minutes total.

Sprinkle one-quarter of the cheese on top of each tortilla, then distribute a scant ½ cup of pork evenly over the top; fold the tortillas in half to cover the filling. (If using store-bought tortillas, which are a bit smaller, spread the cheese and pork over the top of one whole tortilla, then top each with a second tortilla.) Pour about 2 tablespoons oil on top of each homemade tortilla, or 1 tablespoon on each store-bought, letting some of the oil run around the edges and onto the pan. Cook, flipping the quesadillas as needed to crisp both sides in the oil and melt the cheese, 6 to 10 minutes total.

Transfer the quesadillas to four plates and add about ¼ cup chicharrónes, if using, to each quesadilla. Garnish with the queso fresco, cilantro, and onions to taste.

CONTINUED

Chicharrónes

Makes about 1½ cups

Chicharrónes

4 ounces pork belly skin (or 8 ounces if you want leftovers for snacking)

2 cups rice bran oil or canola oil

Kosher salt

Salsa Para Quesadillas

3 medium tomatillos, husked and rinsed

½ white onion

3 cloves garlic

5 dried guajillo chiles, seeded

4 dried cascabel chiles, seeded

Salt

Fill a small pot three-quarters full with water and bring to a boil. Season with salt, then submerge the pork belly skin in the water for one minute. Remove and cut into 1-inch squares.

Preheat the oven to a very low setting (150°F to 200°F). Transfer the pork skin pieces to a large baking sheet and bake until dry, 4 to 6 hours. (The longer they stay in the oven, the puffier and crispier they will be.) Let cool completely.

When ready to serve, set a paper towel–lined plate next to the stove. Fill a small deep-fryer or cast-iron pot with the oil at least several inches deep; heat until the oil registers 350°F on a deep-fat thermometer. Working in batches of about 8 pieces, add some of the pork belly skin to the oil and cook, pulling the chicharrónes up out of the oil with a slotted spoon every few seconds, then dunking them back in, until puffy and crisp, about 3 minutes total. Transfer to the prepared plate and season immediately with salt. Repeat with the remaining pieces of pork belly skin.

Salsa Para Quesadillas

Makes about 3 cups

Preheat the oven to 350°F. Place the tomatillos, onion, and garlic on a baking sheet and roast until the tomatillos are lightly charred, about 30 minutes.

On a griddle or medium skillet over medium-high heat, toast the chiles, turning them every few seconds, until lightly charred but not burned, about 1 minute.

Transfer all of the chiles to a heatproof bowl and cover with boiling water; let sit until very soft, about 20 minutes.

Remove the chiles (discard the soaking water) and grind to a thick paste using a mortar and pestle or a food processor; add the tomatillos, onion, and garlic and continue grinding or processing until chunky. Season with salt to taste.

This taco is inspired by the Yucatán, where the dish called *cochinita pibil* (pork cooked under the ground) originated. At Nopalito, we braise the pork in the oven, first marinating the meat in a traditional red sauce that contains tomatoes, citrus, and spices, including annatto seed—or, in preground paste form, achiote—which gives the slow-cooked meat its deep red color and a nutty, peppery flavor (see page 26 for more on annatto and achiote).

Though the spices and seasonings will go a long way to flavor the pork, wrapping the meat in a banana leaf adds a subtle sweetness and earthy, grassy flavor, and it is worth seeking one out at a Mexican market or online. The same goes for epazote, a pungent herb native to Mexico that you can also find in Mexican markets. But in a pinch, you can substitute basil or cilantro, and leave out the banana leaf.

TACOS DE COCHINITA

Marinated Shredded Pork Tacos ○ Serves 6 to 8

Season the pork generously with salt, then marinate it with the recado rojo for at least 4 hours or up to overnight.

If using the banana leaf, heat a griddle or large skillet to medium heat and briefly cook the leaf, turning once and rotating as needed, until lightly toasted and softened, about 5 seconds per side. Transfer to a small roasting pan allowing it to hang off the side.

Preheat the oven to 300°F. In a medium bowl, combine the tomatoes, orange juice, and lime juice. Place the pork in the roasting pan (laying it atop half of the banana leaf, if using), then pour the tomato mixture over the top. Distribute the onion, garlic, bay leaves, and epazote in the pan, and fold the banana leaf over the pork to cover; cover the pan with foil. Place in the oven and let braise until the meat is very tender, about 3 hours. Remove from the oven and let cool slightly, then shred the meat into small pieces. Taste and adjust the seasoning as needed.

Top each tortilla with as much meat as you like. Garnish with cilantro and onions, and Habanero salsa to taste, keeping in mind that the salsa is quite spicy.

Pork

5 pounds boneless pork shoulder

Kosher salt

Recado Rojo (recipe follows)

1 banana leaf (optional)

1 cup (8 ounces) canned diced tomatoes and their juices

½ cup freshly squeezed orange juice (from 1 to 2 oranges)

½ cup freshly squeezed lime juice (from about 4 limes)

½ white onion

5 cloves garlic

2 bay leaves

¼ bunch fresh epazote, basil, or cilantro

For serving

16 to 20 warm homemade soft corn tortillas (see page 16) or store-bought soft corn tortillas

Fresh cilantro

Thinly sliced red onions

Habanero Salsa (page 221)

CONTINUED

¼ cup plus 1 tablespoon annatto seeds (achiote)

1½ teaspoons dried oregano

1½ teaspoons freshly ground black pepper

1½ teaspoons ground cumin

½ teaspoon ground cinnamon

5 cloves garlic, peeled

1 dried ancho chile, stemmed and seeded

½ teaspoon white vinegar

⅓ cup plus 1 tablespoon freshly squeezed orange juice (from about 1 orange)

¼ cup freshly squeezed lime juice (from about 2 limes)

2 teaspoons rice bran oil or canola oil

Kosher salt

Recado Rojo

Makes 2 cups

Place the annatto seeds in a small pot and cover with water. Bring to a boil, then turn off the heat and let sit for 1 hour.

Meanwhile, preheat the oven to 350°F. Distribute the oregano, pepper, cumin, cinnamon, and garlic on a small baking sheet. Bake, stirring the spices around on the baking sheet halfway through, until the mixture is toasted and aromatic, about 20 minutes.

In a medium heatproof bowl, cover the ancho chile with boiling water; let sit until softened, about 20 minutes, then strain.

Using a slotted spoon, transfer the annatto seeds to a blender (reserve the soaking water). Add the toasted spices, chile, vinegar, orange and lime juices, and a generous pinch of salt. Blend, streaming in the oil to form a thick, smooth paste and adding some of the soaking water from the achiote as needed.

The traditional preparation for *tacos al pastor* is a spectacle that would make anyone hungry. A large piece of pork such as a shoulder cut is marinated in a paste of dried spices, then topped with pineapple and set on a spit to roast low and slow. Thin pieces of the pork are then sliced off and served in tacos. We have so much pork on our restaurant menu that we decided to try the traditional al pastor seasonings with seared fish, and the results were just as satisfying.

This recipe for the adobo makes extra, as it will keep in the fridge for 1 to 2 weeks and can be used throughout the week as a rub for beef, pork, chicken, or shrimp, or stirred into scrambled eggs. For best results, choose a hearty, not flaky, white fish such as snapper that won't fall apart during cooking and can soak up all the adobo.

1 pound skinless snapper cod, or halibut fillets

Salt

2 tablespoons Adobo Paste (recipe follows)

Rice bran oil or canola oil, for sautéing

Adobo Paste

8 dried ancho chiles

3 dried puya chiles

4 cloves garlic

1 tablespoon cumin seeds

½ tablespoon dried thyme

½ tablespoon dried oregano

1 tablespoon Nopalito Spices (page 35) or ground chili powder

2 jalapeños

½ bunch fresh cilantro

For serving

8 warm homemade soft corn tortillas (see page 16) or store-bought soft corn tortillas

Diced white onion

Chopped fresh cilantro

Small orange wedges or finely chopped pineapple

Salsa de Morita con Tomatillo (page 221)

TACOS DE PESCADO AL PASTOR

Fish Tacos Marinated in Adobo ○ Makes 8

Cut the fish into thin 2-ounce pieces (about 5 inches long); season with salt and coat with the adobo. Cover and let marinate at least 2 hours and up to overnight.

In a large skillet or on a griddle, heat 2 to 3 tablespoons oil over medium-high heat. Once the oil is hot, add the fish and cook until seared on one side, about 3 minutes. Turn and cook on the remaining side until just cooked through, about 3 minutes more.

Divide the fish among the warm tortillas. Garnish with the onions, cilantro, oranges, and salsa.

Adobo Paste

Makes about 1½ cups

Preheat a griddle or skillet over medium heat. Add all of the dried chiles and let toast, turning them every 10 seconds, until you can smell them and the color has slightly changed, about 1 minute total. Transfer the chiles to a medium bowl and cover with boiling water; let sit until soft, about 20 minutes.

Meanwhile, preheat the oven to 350°F. Place the garlic and all of the dried herbs and spices on a baking sheet and bake, stirring the spices around on the baking sheet halfway through, until toasted and aromatic, about 10 minutes.

Transfer the spices and chiles to a blender (reserve the soaking water). Add the fresh jalapeños and the cilantro. Starting with no soaking water and adding small amounts only as needed, blend until the mixture forms a smooth paste.

In Mexico, the *tamal*—a collection of corn masa and sometimes other fillings wrapped in a corn husk, banana leaf, or other package—is just like a taco or any antojito in that the filling can change with the season, region, or occasion. Sweet potato is our seasonal choice for fall at the restaurant, and it pairs really well with a spicy-sweet mole. Be sure to prepare the mole before you get started on the tamales.

Achieving the balance of flavors in a mole is a bit like blending paint colors, which is why the best versions have many ingredients. Here, a *mole amarillo* ("yellow mole") gets its color from a combination of dark and red chiles, bright red fresh tomatoes, and green tomatillos. This recipe makes extra so that the next few times you crave mole to use atop chicken, fish, pork, veggies, or enchiladas, you will have it at your fingertips—no spice blending required.

2 medium whole sweet potatoes, peeled, plus 6 cups ½-inch-diced sweet potatoes

Olive oil

7 cups Homemade Masa (page 12) or masa prepared from store-bought masa harina

3 cups (6 sticks) unsalted butter, softened

1 tablespoon kosher salt, plus more as needed

1 teaspoon baking powder

½ white onion, chopped

1 jalapeño, thinly sliced

1 clove garlic, peeled and chopped

2 cups Mole Amarillo (recipe follows)

20 large corn husks or 40 small ones

CONTINUED

TAMALES DE AMARILLO CON CAMOTE

Sweet Potato Tamales with Mole Amarillo ○ Makes about 24

To make the filling, preheat the oven to 350°F. Rub the whole sweet potatoes with olive oil and wrap them together in foil; place on a large baking sheet and bake until extremely soft, about 1 hour 15 minutes. About halfway through baking, place the diced sweet potatoes on the baking sheet and roast until al dente, 20 to 30 minutes.

Quarter the whole sweet potatoes and puree in a food processor.

Place 1 cup of the puree in the bowl of a stand mixer fitted with the paddle attachment. Add half each of the masa, butter, salt, and baking powder and beat until well combined. (Alternatively, you can mix the ingredients by hand, but the stand mixer creates an airier result.) Transfer this mixture to a larger bowl, then repeat the mixer processing with another 1 cup of the potato puree and the remaining masa, butter, salt, and baking powder. Combine with the first batch, then taste and adjust the seasoning as needed (it should taste well-seasoned). Discard any remaining potato puree or save for another use.

To make the chunky sweet potato filling, in a medium skillet, heat 1 tablespoon olive oil over high heat. Add the onion, jalapeño, and garlic and season with salt; cook, stirring occasionally, until the onions are translucent, 4 to 5 minutes. (Turn down the heat as needed so the onions don't start to brown.)

In a large mixing bowl, combine the onion mixture, the roasted diced potatoes, and 2 cups of the mole amarillo. Taste and add more salt as needed.

To make the tamales, soak the corn husks in very hot water until softened, about 20 minutes. Remove from the water (no need to dry them off). Working with one at a time, lay a husk on a clean work surface with the curved side facing up and the narrower end facing you. (Some husks will be smaller than others—if necessary, use two small husks together, overlapping

CONTINUED

Mole Amarillo

5 dried guajillo chiles, stemmed and seeded

2 dried ancho chiles, stemmed and seeded

3 dried morita chiles, stemmed

5 whole cloves

4 bay leaves

1½ teaspoons cumin seeds

1½ teaspoons ground dried pimiento

1½ teaspoons ground allspice

1 cup rice bran oil or canola oil, divided

½ white onion, chopped

2 cloves garlic, chopped

½ jalapeño, stemmed

Salt

1 cup (8 ounces) diced canned tomatoes and their juices

10 medium tomatillos, husked and rinsed

½ cup raw unsalted pepitas (pumpkin seeds)

½ cup unsalted peanuts

½ cup Homemade Masa (page 12) or masa prepared from store-bought masa harina

their long edges slightly.) Using a spoon or your hands and leaving a 1½-inch border clear along the wide, flat end of the husks, place a heaping ¼ cup of masa over the center of each corn husk. Spread the masa out to form a round about 3 inches across. Add about ¼ cup of the chunky sweet potato filling in a line down the center of the masa, then fold the long edges of the corn husk over the filling to cover. Finally, fold the pointy end of the husk over to form a packet (the opposite end of the tamal should remain open). Tamales can be filled up to 2 days in advance of steaming. You can also freeze them at this point; add an extra 15 minutes of steaming time if starting with frozen ones.

Transfer the tamales to a steamer, piling them as needed to fit, either horizontally or with their open ends facing up. Steam until the masa has firmed, 60 to 90 minutes. (To test, open the husk: a toothpick inserted into the masa should come out mostly clean.)

Mole Amarillo

Makes 6 cups

Preheat the oven to 350°F. Put all of the chiles on a baking sheet and roast for 5 minutes. Remove the chiles but do not turn off the oven. Transfer the chiles to a medium heatproof bowl; cover with boiling water and let sit until softened, about 20 minutes.

On the same baking sheet, spread out the cloves, bay leaves, cumin, pimiento, and allspice. Bake, stirring the spices around on the baking sheet halfway through baking, until toasted and aromatic, about 10 minutes.

In a medium pot, heat ¼ cup of the oil over medium-high heat. Add the onion, garlic, and jalapeño, and lower the heat to medium; season with salt and cook, stirring occasionally, until the vegetables are very soft and the onions are translucent, 10 to 15 minutes. Add the tomatoes and bring to a simmer; cook, stirring occasionally, about 30 minutes.

Transfer the tomato-onion mixture to a blender, then add the spices, tomatillos, pepitas, peanuts, reconstituted chiles (reserve the soaking water), and a generous pinch of salt. Blend, adding some of the soaking water as needed, until smooth.

In a large pot, heat the remaining ¾ cup oil until hot. Turn off the heat and add the tomato-onion mixture quickly and all at once (be careful, as the mixture will splatter). Bring the mixture to a boil. Reduce to a simmer and let cook for about 2 hours. Taste and add more salt if needed.

In a clean blender, working in batches if needed, combine the masa with about 1 cup water and blend until very liquidy. Pour it slowly into the tomato mixture and let cook for another 30 minutes. Taste and add more salt as needed. The mole can be cooled fully and stored at this point for up to 5 days.

Birria is a stew from Jalisco, in western Mexico, that, similar to a mole, contains a wide assortment of dried chiles and spices. Classically, birria was cooked underground on a fire covered with stones and agave leaves, and it was often made with goat or lamb meat. In this version, you braise chicken in the traditional flavors of birria, then use it to fill tamales.

Luckily, birria is a little less complicated to make than mole, with fewer ingredients. And to make the recipe even more manageable, you can prepare the chile paste, cook the chicken, or even fill the tamales in advance, then steam them the next day.

One of the secrets to moist, flavorful tamales is using a decent amount of fat. For meat-filled tamales, it's traditional to mix the masa with lard, but you can also use butter, which I do when I make vegetarian tamales. It may seem like a lot of fat, but don't worry: part of it drains out as the tamales steam.

TAMALES DE BIRRIA CON POLLO

Tamales with Stewed Chicken   ◎   Makes about 24

To prepare the chicken, place it in a large pot and add enough water to just cover it. Add the onion, garlic, and bay leaves and bring to a boil, then reduce to a simmer and let cook, skimming the foam and fat off the top occasionally, until the meat is just cooked through, about 45 minutes. Remove the chicken (reserve the cooking liquid for another use if desired) and let cool slightly; finely shred the meat into small pieces. Set aside or refrigerate until ready to use.

Preheat the oven to 350°F. Place all of the dried chiles in a medium heatproof bowl and cover with boiling water; let sit until the chiles are softened, about 20 minutes. Meanwhile, combine the cinnamon, cumin, thyme, ginger, marjoram, cloves, allspice, and sesame seeds on a baking sheet and bake until toasted, about 10 minutes.

Transfer the spices and the softened chiles (discard the soaking water) to a blender. Add the tomatoes and vinegar and blend until smooth. Pour the mixture into a large pot and bring to a boil; reduce to a simmer and let cook for 30 minutes.

When you're ready to assemble the tamales, fry the salsa: In a large pot, heat the oil over high heat. Pour in the salsa quickly and all at once (be careful, as the oil may splatter) and bring to a boil; add the chocolate and season with salt. The mixture should be thin; if necessary, add some of the reserved chicken cooking liquid or water. The salsa can be prepared to this point up to 3 days in advance if then cooled completely and refrigerated.

Combine the chicken with just enough salsa to cover and saturate it. Reserve the remaining salsa for serving alongside the tamales.

Chicken Filling

1 whole (3- to 3½-pound) chicken

½ white onion

3 cloves garlic

5 bay leaves

7 dried guajillo chiles, stemmed and seeded

12 dried chiles de árbol, stemmed and seeded

½ cinnamon stick

½ teaspoon cumin seeds

½ teaspoon dried thyme

½ teaspoon ground ginger

½ teaspoon dried marjoram

5 whole cloves

5 allspice berries

1 tablespoon sesame seeds

3 cups (24 ounces) canned diced tomatoes and their juices

¼ cup white vinegar

CONTINUED

CONTINUED

¼ cup rice bran oil
or canola oil

1½ ounces (half a 3.1-ounce
disk) Mexican chocolate
(preferably Ibarra or
Abuelita brand), chopped

Salt

Tamales

6 cups Homemade Masa
(page 12) or masa prepared
from store-bought masa
harina

2 cups lard or softened
unsalted butter (4 sticks)

1 teaspoon baking powder

1 tablespoon kosher salt,
plus more as needed

24 large corn husks or
48 small ones

To make the tamales, in the bowl of a stand mixer fitted with the paddle attachment, combine the masa, lard, baking powder, and salt; beat until well blended. (Alternatively, you can stir the ingredients by hand in a large bowl, but the mixer will make the masa lighter and airier.)

To assemble, soak the corn husks in very hot water until softened, about 20 minutes. Remove from the water (no need to dry them off). Working with one at a time, lay a husk on a clean work surface with the curved side facing up and the narrower end facing you. (Some husks will be smaller than others—if necessary, use two small husks together, overlapping their long edges slightly.) Using a spoon or your hands and leaving a 1½-inch border clear along the wide, flat end of the husk, place a heaping ¼ cup of masa in the center of the corn husk, then spread it to form a circle about 3 inches across. Add about ¼ cup of the chicken filling to the center of the masa, then fold the long edges of the corn husk over the filling to cover. Fold the pointy end of the husk over to form a packet (the opposite end of the tamal should remain open). Tamales can be filled up to 2 days in advance of steaming. You can also freeze them at this point; add an extra 15 minutes of steaming time if starting with frozen ones.

Transfer the tamales to a steamer, piling them as needed to fit, either horizontally or with their open ends facing up. Steam until the masa has firmed, 60 to 90 minutes. (To test, open the husk: a toothpick inserted into the masa should come out mostly clean.)

To serve, open the tamales and spoon some of the extra salsa on top if desired.

These Pueblan tamales get their name from *pipián*, a mole or complex sauce containing different kinds of seeds such as pepita, sunflower, or sesame. The seeds add a richer texture and nutty flavor to what would otherwise be a simple tomato-based salsa.

You can garnish these tamales as you like, adding crumbled queso fresco, a drizzle of crema or sour cream, or more toasted pepita or sesame seeds, or just serve them on their own. Extras will keep for weeks in the freezer.

TAMALES EMPIPIANADOS

Tamales with Red Spiced Sunflower Seed Mole   ○   Makes about 24

To make the tamales, in the bowl of a stand mixer fitted with the paddle attachment, combine the masa, lard, baking powder, and salt until well mixed. (Alternatively, you can stir the ingredients by hand in a large bowl, but the mixer will make the masa lighter and airier.) Set aside.

To prepare the chicken, place it in a large pot and add enough water to just cover it. Add the onion, garlic, bay leaves, and a few generous pinches of salt. Bring to a boil, then reduce to a steady simmer and let cook, skimming the foam and fat off the top as needed, until the meat is just cooked through, about 45 minutes. Remove the chicken, and strain and reserve the cooking liquid. Finely shred the meat from the bones and set aside or refrigerate until ready to use. Preheat the oven to 350°F.

To make the pipián, heat a griddle or small skillet over medium heat, then add all of the dried chiles; cook, turning occasionally, until you can smell them and their color has darkened slightly, about 1 minute. Transfer to a medium heatproof bowl and cover with boiling water; let sit until soft, about 20 minutes (reserve in their soaking water until ready to use).

Meanwhile, combine the cloves, cumin, allspice, sunflower seeds, and sesame seeds on a baking sheet. Bake until toasted, stirring once halfway through, 10 to 15 minutes.

Transfer the spices and seeds, the chiles and about ½ cup of their soaking water (reserve the rest of the water), and the tomatoes to a blender; season generously with salt and blend until the mixture has a coarse consistency.

To complete the pipián, in a large pot, heat the lard over high heat. Stir in the contents of the blender. Bring to a boil, then reduce to a simmer; let cook for 30 minutes, adding a little more soaking water if needed to achieve a thick, grainy consistency.

In a large bowl, combine the chicken and 4 cups of the pipián. (Reserve the remaining pipián for serving.) Taste and add more salt as needed.

To assemble the tamales, soak the corn husks in very hot water until softened, about 20 minutes. Remove from the water (no need to dry them off). Working with one at a time, lay a husk on a clean work surface with the curved side facing up and the narrower end facing you. (Some husks will be smaller than others—if necessary, use two small husks

Tamales

6 cups Homemade Masa (page 12) or masa prepared from store-bought masa harina

2 cups lard or softened unsalted butter (4 sticks)

1 teaspoon baking powder

1 tablespoon kosher salt, plus more as needed

24 large corn husks or 48 small ones

Chicken Filling

1 whole (3- to 3½-pound) chicken

½ white onion

3 cloves garlic

2 bay leaves

Kosher salt

4 dried guajillo chiles, stemmed and seeded

3 dried ancho chiles, stemmed and seeded

¾ teaspoon ground cloves

¾ teaspoon ground cumin

¾ teaspoon ground allspice

¾ cup raw sunflower seeds

¼ cup plus 2 tablespoons sesame seeds

4 cups canned diced tomatoes and their juices

6 cups water

¼ cup lard or unsalted butter

For serving (optional)

Crumbled Cotija cheese or queso fresco

Crema (page 35) or sour cream

Toasted pepitas

Toasted sesame seeds

together, overlapping their long edges slightly.) Using a spoon or your hands and leaving a 1½-inch border clear along the wide, flat end of the husk, place a heaping ¼ cup of masa over the center of each corn husk. Spread the masa out to form a round about 3 inches across. Place about ¼ cup of the chicken filling down the center of the masa, then fold the long edges of the husk over the filling to cover. Fold the pointy end of the husk over to form a packet (the opposite end of the tamal should remain open). Tamales can be filled up to 2 days in advance of steaming. You can also freeze them at this point; add an extra 15 minutes of steaming time if starting with frozen ones.

Transfer the tamales to a steamer, piling them as needed to fit, either horizontally or with their open ends facing up. Steam until the masa has firmed, 60 to 90 minutes. (To test, open the husk: a toothpick inserted into the masa should come out mostly clean.)

To serve, open the tamales and spoon some of the pipián on top. Sprinkle with Cotija cheese, crema, toasted pepitas, and/or toasted sesame seeds if desired.

How to Reheat Tamales

Making tamales can be a bit laborious, but making one big batch will guarantee leftovers. Once they've been steamed, you can store them covered in the refrigerator or freezer, then reheat them at will. Just as the best ears of grilled corn are the ones where the pieces take on a little char from the fire, the best tamales are those that are seared on both sides on a medium-hot griddle or pan (no oil necessary). You don't want them to burn on the bottom while the centers are still cold, but a little blackening is okay and will add a layer of fire-kissed flavor. Remove after a few minutes, when a toothpick inserted into the center of the masa comes out mostly clean.

There are so many types of empanadas in Mexico—the details depend on the region you're in. Some are sweet, made with flour and sugar; others are savory, featuring a pastry made with masa and usually lard and salt. This version features tender beef brisket braised simply with garlic, onion, and bay leaves, then shredded and used as a filling. The longer you cook the beef, the more tender it will be, but since you mix it with salsa, it will be moist no matter what.

You can prepare the filling and the masa pastry in advance, but you really have to fry these empanadas just before eating. Adding baking powder and using an electric mixer are two secrets to guaranteeing a light, puffy pastry.

EMPANADAS DE DESHEBRADA DE RES

Fried Beef Empanadas   ○   Makes 8

To make the beef, place the beef in a small pot and cover with water. Add the onion, garlic, and bay leaf; season with salt. Bring to a boil, then reduce to a simmer and let cook until tender, about 1½ hours. Let cool slightly. Remove the meat and finely shred it. The meat can be prepared up to 2 days in advance. Store it in the cooking liquid and refrigerate.

In the bowl of a stand mixer fitted with the paddle attachment, mix the masa with the lard and baking powder until well combined. (Alternatively, you can stir the ingredients by hand in a large bowl, but the mixer will produce a lighter, airier masa.)

To make the filling, in a medium pot, bring the salsa to a boil; reduce to a simmer and let cook for 10 minutes. Turn off the heat and let cool slightly, then mix with the shredded beef, starting with less than ½ cup of salsa if you like it less spicy.

To form the empanadas, line a tortilla press with a large round of plastic cut from a plastic bag. Scoop ¼ cup of the masa dough and form it into a ball, then flatten the ball slightly into a disk. Place the disk in the center of the tortilla press, then top with another round of plastic. Close the tortilla press but not all the way, to form a large round slightly thicker than a tortilla (about ⅛ inch thick when raw; the dough will expand in the fryer). (If not using a tortilla press, roll out the masa between two pieces of plastic using a rolling pin.) Remove the top piece of plastic and place some of the beef filling (a heaping ¼ cup) on the center of the round, leaving a generous border. Using the remaining piece of plastic, carefully fold the empanada shell in half to cover the filling and form a half-moon shape. Press the joined edges of the pastry to seal tightly. Transfer to a baking sheet or platter and repeat with the remaining masa and filling.

Set a plate lined with paper towels next to the stove. In a 12-inch skillet, heat the oil until it registers 350°F on a deep-fat thermometer. Working in batches as needed, carefully place the empanadas in the pan; let cook until lightly browned, about 4 minutes, then turn and repeat. Transfer to the prepared plate. Serve hot garnished with the salsa, cabbage, crema, queso fresco, onion, and cilantro.

Filling

1 pound beef shoulder

¼ large white onion

2 cloves garlic

1 bay leaf

Salt

½ cup (4 ounces) Salsa Frita de Guajillo (page 227), plus more per serving

Masa

2 cups Homemade Masa (page 12) or masa prepared from store-bought masa harina

2 tablespoons lard or softened unsalted butter

½ teaspoon baking powder

For Frying and Serving

4 cups rice bran oil or canola oil

Thinly sliced green cabbage (optional)

Crema (page 35) or sour cream (optional)

Queso fresco (optional)

Finely chopped white onion (optional)

Chopped fresh cilantro leaves (optional)

Think of everything that comes to mind when you hear the word *empanada*—"greasy," "heavy," "beef-filled"—then erase it. This coastal-inspired version from the region of Nayarit, Mexico, features sweet, delicate shrimp and a chopped vegetable mixture. In addition to the unexpected seafood filling, these empanadas are different in that their corn-based fried pastry shell contains guajillo adobo, a paste made with blended dried chiles, which happens to go really well with the shrimp.

For the cleanest flavor, always look for fresh wild shrimp rather than farmed or frozen.

Guajillo Adobo (Chile Paste)

4 dried guajillo chiles, stemmed and seeded

Filling

3 tablespoons rice bran oil or canola oil

½ white onion, finely chopped

2 cloves garlic, finely chopped

1 jalapeño, finely chopped

Salt

2 cups (16 ounces) pureed canned tomatoes

1 cup cleaned raw shrimp, coarsely chopped (from about 1½ pounds)

Masa

2 cups Homemade Masa (page 12) or masa prepared from store-bought masa harina

2 tablespoons lard or softened unsalted butter

½ teaspoon baking powder

For Frying and Serving

2 cups rice bran oil or canola oil

Salsa de Tomatillo y Jalapeño (page 227; optional)

Thinly sliced green cabbage (optional)

Crema (page 35) or sour cream (optional)

Finely chopped white onion (optional)

Chopped cilantro leaves (optional)

EMPANADAS DE CAMARÓN

Fried White Shrimp Empanadas   ○   Makes 8

Cover the chiles with boiling water; let sit until softened, about 20 minutes.

Meanwhile, to make the filling, heat the oil in a large skillet over high heat. Add the onions, garlic, and jalapeño and season with salt; reduce the heat to low, then cook, stirring occasionally, until the vegetables are very soft, about 15 minutes. Add the tomatoes and bring to a boil over medium-high heat. Reduce to a simmer; add the shrimp and smash it into the sauce with the tip of a wooden spoon. Let cook until the shrimp has turned pink, 3 to 5 minutes, then remove the pan from the heat.

To make the guajillo adobo, remove the chiles from their soaking water (reserve the water) and transfer to a small blender; puree, adding a little of the soaking water if needed to blend, until the mixture forms a smooth, thick paste.

In a stand mixer fitted with the paddle attachment, beat the masa, ¼ cup of adobo, the lard, and the baking powder until combined. (You can stir by hand, but the mixer will make it light and fluffy.)

To form the empanadas, line the bottom of a tortilla press with a large round of plastic cut from a plastic bag. Form ¼ cup of masa into a small ball, then flatten the ball slightly. Place in the center of the tortilla press, then top with another round of plastic. Close the press down evenly but not all the way, to form a large round slightly thicker than a tortilla (about ⅛ inch thick when raw; the dough will expand in the fryer). (If not using a tortilla press, roll out the masa between two pieces of plastic using a rolling pin.) Remove the top piece of plastic and place ¼ cup of the shrimp filling on the center of the round. Using the remaining piece of plastic, carefully fold the empanada shell in half to cover the filling. Press the edges of the pastry to seal tightly. Transfer to a baking sheet and repeat with the remaining masa and filling.

Set a paper towel–lined plate next to the stove. In a 12-inch skillet, heat the oil until it registers 350°F on a deep-fat thermometer. Carefully place an empanada in the pan; let cook until lightly browned, about 2 minutes, then turn and repeat on the other side. Transfer to the prepared plate. Repeat with the remaining empanadas. Serve with the salsa, cabbage, crema, onion, and cilantro, if desired.

Zucchini grows like crazy in the south of Mexico due to the year-round hot weather. Growing up, we had a huge patch in our backyard, and when the blossoms were plentiful, we'd stuff them inside airy fried corn empanadas.

The combination of fresh masa and delicate vegetables makes these empanadas taste particularly light and summery. One makes a great snack on its own, but make a few extras—you won't want to stop at just one.

EMPANADAS DE FLOR DE CALABAZA

Fried Empanadas with Squash Blossoms ○ Makes 8

Filling

¼ cup extra-virgin olive oil

½ white onion, finely chopped

½ jalapeño, finely chopped

1 medium zucchini, finely diced

6 squash blossoms, rinsed, dried, and quartered

Kosher salt and freshly ground black pepper

Salsa

½ cup extra-virgin olive oil

6 dried chiles de árbol, stemmed and seeded

3 Roma (plum) tomatoes, coarsely chopped

Kosher salt and freshly ground black pepper

Masa

2 cups Homemade Masa (page 12) or masa prepared from store-bought masa harina

2 tablespoons lard or softened unsalted butter

½ teaspoon baking powder

For Frying and Serving

2 cups rice bran oil or canola oil

Thinly sliced green cabbage

Crumbled queso fresco

Chopped fresh cilantro leaves

To make the filling, in a large pot or Dutch oven, heat the olive oil over medium heat. Add the onion and jalapeño and cook, stirring occasionally, until the onion is translucent, about 3 minutes. Add the zucchini and cook, stirring occasionally, until tender, 3 to 5 minutes. Add the squash blossoms and cook for 1 minute. Season to taste with salt and pepper.

To make the salsa, in a medium skillet, heat the olive oil over medium heat. Add the chiles and fry until lightly browned, about 30 seconds. Stir in the tomatoes and cook until thickened slightly, about 10 minutes; season with salt and pepper. Transfer to a molcajete or a blender, and grind or blend until smooth. Taste and adjust the seasoning as necessary.

In the bowl of a stand mixer fitted with the paddle attachment, mix the masa with the lard and baking powder until well combined. (Alternatively, you can stir the ingredients by hand in a large bowl, but the mixer will produce a lighter, airier masa.)

To form the empanadas, divide the masa into 8 equal balls (2 ounces each). One at a time, using a tortilla press lined on the top and bottom with plastic wrap, flatten each ball into a round tortilla. (Alternatively, you can place each ball of masa between two sheets of plastic wrap and roll it out with a rolling pin.) Place ¼ cup filling on one half of the tortilla. Fold the opposite half over to form a half-moon shape, and pinch the edges together to seal. Repeat with the remaining masa and filling.

Set a plate lined with paper towels next to the stove. In a large, deep skillet or sauté pan, add enough oil to reach 1 inch up the sides, and heat over medium heat until shimmering. Add the empanadas, in batches if necessary to avoid crowding, and fry, turning once, until golden brown on each side, about 6 minutes total. Using a slotted metal spatula, transfer to the prepared plate to drain some of the oil.

Serve hot with the salsa, cabbage, queso fresco, and cilantro.

There is something exciting about the many ways you can use a simple masa to create different forms, shapes, and flavors. A gordita is one of many examples, made by puffing up a rounder, thicker tortilla, then opening it up to form a pocket—sort of like a pita bread.

A mixture of potato and chorizo is one of the most popular and classic gordita fillings in Mexico. Because chorizo is so strongly spiced and has some heat of its own, I prefer a milder salsa with this dish. Its real job is to provide a little tanginess to cut through the meaty sausage and starchy potatoes.

Filling and Cooking

1 tablespoon kosher salt

1 cup peeled, diced russet potatoes (from about 1 medium-to-large potato)

Rice bran oil or canola oil, for griddling

1 cup Chorizo Oaxaqueño (page 44) or crumbled store-bought Mexican chorizo, casings removed

Masa

3 cups Homemade Masa (page 12) or masa prepared from store-bought masa harina

1 tablespoon lard or softened unsalted butter

For serving

Salsa de Árbol (page 233)

Queso fresco

Thinly sliced cabbage

Chopped fresh cilantro

Diced white onion

GORDITAS DE PAPAS CON CHORIZO

Potato Gorditas with Chorizo ○ Makes 8

Bring a small pot of water to a boil; add the salt and potatoes, and let cook until al dente, 6 to 8 minutes. Drain and set aside.

In a medium bowl, mix the masa with the lard until well combined. Form the masa into 8 equal balls, a little less than ¼ cup each, then flatten each ball slightly. In a tortilla press lined on both sides with a round of plastic, flatten each masa ball into a round slightly thicker than a tortilla (between ⅛ and ¼ inch thick, and 4 inches wide).

In a large skillet or griddle over medium heat, drizzle in about 1 teaspoon oil for each tortilla, and add as many tortillas as you can without overlapping them. Cook, turning once, until puffed up and filled with air, 3 to 4 minutes per side. Remove and let cool slightly. Using a paring knife or butter knife, pierce the edge of each gordita horizontally, then carefully wiggle the knife between the layers, separating them and creating an opening in the top third of the gordita (it should look like a coin purse).

When ready to serve, in a large skillet or griddle over medium-high heat, drizzle in 1 to 2 teaspoons oil and add a gordita; cook, turning once or twice, until lightly crispy on both sides, about 4 minutes total. Repeat with the remaining gorditas, adding more oil to the pan as needed.

Meanwhile, in a separate medium skillet, cook the chorizo, stirring occasionally, until cooked through and hot, about 6 minutes. Stir in the potatoes and cook until hot and tender. Divide the mixture among the gorditas, stuffing ¼ cup of it into each pocket. Garnish with the salsa de árbol, queso fresco, cabbage, cilantro, and onion.

When I started a Mexican restaurant in San Francisco, I was happy to discover a tradition from home that is alive and well here, too: the harvesting of *huitlacoche*, a rare fungus that occurs naturally but randomly on corn cobs and is therefore considered a delicacy to find and eat. Since there is no way to deliberately grow it, and it grows in only certain humid conditions, huitlacoche is nicknamed "corn truffle." This ingredient is truly unique to old-school southern Mexican cooking, and most Mexican American restaurants don't serve it. The lucky thing is, you can also find huitlacoche (also called corn smut) frozen in Mexican markets or buy it online. Eating it is an experience worth having and sharing with friends.

Their sandal shape earns these antojitos the name *huaraches*. They are significantly thicker than tortillas, so one or two per person is all you need for a meal.

HUARACHES DE HUITLACOCHE Y HONGOS

Blue Corn Huaraches with "Corn Truffle" and Mushrooms   ○   Serves 4

¼ cup plus 3 tablespoons rice bran oil or canola oil

2 cloves garlic

1 jalapeño, diced

½ white onion, diced

¼ cup frozen huitlacoche, thawed and finely chopped

2 cups king oyster or hen of the woods mushrooms, or a blend, coarsely broken

Salt

4 leaves epazote or fresh basil, torn

2 cups Homemade Masa (page 12) or masa prepared from store-bought masa harina

½ cup Frijoles Pinquitos Refritos (page 126) or good-quality store-bought refried pinto beans

For serving

Salsa de Árbol (page 233)

Crema (page 35) or sour cream

Queso fresco

Chopped white onion

Fresh cilantro

In a medium pot over medium-high heat, heat 2 tablespoons of the oil and the garlic, jalapeño, and onion; turn the heat down to medium and cook, stirring occasionally, until the onion is translucent, about 5 minutes. Add the huitlacoche and cook, stirring occasionally, 20 minutes.

Meanwhile, in a large skillet, heat 1 tablespoon of the oil over high heat. Add the mushrooms and season with salt; cook, stirring occasionally, until most of the moisture evaporates and the mushrooms are browned in places, 5 minutes. Combine with the huitlacoche mixture and adjust the seasoning as needed. Sprinkle with the epazote. Keep warm.

Working with ½ cup of the masa at a time, form the masa into a little cup in the palm of your hand. Put about 2 tablespoons of the refried beans in the center of the cup, then close the masa up around the beans, rolling it gently in your hands to help blend and distribute the beans slightly. Form the masa into a small oblong patty (about 5 inches long). In a tortilla press lined on the top and bottom with a round of plastic cut from a plastic bag, press the masa to form about a ¼-inch-thick, 3- to 4-inch-wide oval (it should look like the sole of a sandal). Do not press the huarache too thin or the beans will leak out.

Preheat a large skillet or griddle to medium-high heat. Carefully add the huaraches to the dry surface, working in batches if necessary, and cook until just set and starting to crisp on each side, 3 to 4 minutes per side. Remove with a spatula, coat the pan lightly with oil (1 to 2 teaspoons per huarache), and cook until lightly crispy, about 2 minutes per side. With the huarache still on the griddle or pan, add the warm mushroom topping. Transfer to a plate and garnish with salsa, crema, queso fresco, onions, and cilantro.

This saucy, tomatoey, spiced ground beef topping is one of the easiest recipes in the book, and one of the most comforting. Before piling it onto crispy tortillas, we smear the tortillas with refried beans to help the toppings stick.

Picadillo comes from the Spanish word *picar*, which means "to chop," since the old-school versions of these tostadas contained hand-chopped beef. Today we use ground beef, since it is so readily available and effortless, and add finely diced carrots and potatoes for color and variety. Stewing the fresh tomatoes with tomato paste and some smoky cumin gives picadillo that cooked-all-day flavor, but this meal will be on your plate in less than 60 minutes. The leftovers will make you happy for days—both kids and grown-ups become obsessed with putting picadillo on everything from tostadas to tacos to chips.

TOSTADAS DE PICADILLO

Ground Beef Tostadas ◦ Makes 12

To make the picadillo, in a medium pot over medium-high heat, add the ground beef and season generously with salt. Cook, stirring occasionally, until no pink remains, about 7 minutes. Stir in the onions, jalapeños, oregano, cumin, tomato paste, and Nopalito spices and cook for 2 minutes more. Add the tomatoes and cook, stirring occasionally, 20 minutes. Add the carrots and potato and cook, stirring occasionally, until the vegetables are cooked through but still al dente, about 20 minutes more.

When ready to serve, quickly warm up the refried beans in a small pot, thinning them as needed with water to achieve a spreadable consistency. Carefully spread some of the bean mixture onto each warm tostada shell. Follow with a mound of picadillo. Garnish with the queso fresco, crema, onions, cabbage, and cilantro.

Picadillo

3 cups ground beef (about 1½ pounds), on the fattier side

Salt

2 cups finely chopped white onion (from about 1 large onion)

1½ to 2 jalapeños, finely chopped

½ teaspoon dried oregano

½ teaspoon ground cumin

¼ cup tomato paste

1 tablespoon Nopalito Spices (page 35) or ground chili pepper

2 cups (16 ounces) canned diced tomatoes and their juices

2 cups finely chopped carrots (from about 4 carrots)

¾ cup finely chopped Yukon gold potato (from about 1 small)

For serving

1 cup (8 ounces) refried beans, for spreading

12 homemade tostada shells (see right) or warmed store-bought tostadas

Crumbled queso fresco

Crema (page 35) or sour cream

Thinly sliced or chopped white onion

Thinly sliced green cabbage

Thinly sliced cilantro

How to Make Your Own Tostada Shells

You can make tostadas—the crispy tortilla base for this dish—one of two ways: by baking day-old, homemade corn tortillas (or store-bought tortillas right from the package) at low heat in the oven to dry them out, or frying them in oil at high heat. Alternatively, you can buy tostadas in stores and reheat according to the package directions.

TO BAKE: Preheat the oven to 300°F. Place the tortillas in a single layer on a rimmed baking sheet. Bake until crispy, 20 to 30 minutes.

TO FRY: To a medium frying pan, add enough rice bran oil or canola oil to reach ½ inch up the sides of the pan. Set a paper towel–lined plate next to the stove. Heat the oil to high heat (but not to the point where it's smoking) and add the tortillas 2 or 3 at a time as space allows. Fry, flipping occasionally, until golden and crisp on both sides. Transfer to the prepared plate to drain.

Tinga is a comforting chipotle-and-tomato-stewed chicken recipe from Puebla that usually has a tangy, lightly smoky flavor. Because of the saturated smokiness, sweetness, and kick of spice from the chipotle peppers, and the toastiness of the corn tostada, you get a lot of flavor in this dish from very few ingredients.

If you like dark chicken meat, feel free to substitute a couple of thighs for one or both of the breasts.

TOSTADAS DE TINGA POBLANA

Chicken Tinga Tostadas   ○   Makes 8

1 large or 2 small dried chipotle chiles

2 raw bone-in, skin-on chicken breasts (about 1 pound) or 3 cups cooked shredded rotisserie chicken

Salt

1 medium white onion, ½ whole, ½ thinly sliced

3 cloves garlic, whole, plus 2 cloves garlic, chopped

1 bay leaf

2 tablespoons rice bran oil or canola oil

1 (15-ounce) can diced tomatoes and their juices

3 tablespoons chopped fresh epazote or cilantro

For serving

1 cup (8 ounces) Frijoles Pinquitos Refritos (page 126) or good-quality store-bought refried pinto beans

8 homemade tostadas (see page 117) or warmed store-bought tostadas

Crema (page 35) or sour cream

Crumbled queso fresco

In a small pot, cover the chile with enough water just to cover; bring to a boil, then turn off the heat and let sit until the chile is softened, about 20 minutes.

Meanwhile, put the chicken breasts in a medium pot and add enough water just to cover; season generously with salt and add the whole ½ of the onion, the whole garlic cloves, and the bay leaf. Bring the water to a boil, then reduce to a steady simmer and cook until the meat is just cooked through, about 30 minutes. Remove the chicken, reserving the liquid for another use if desired, and let cool slightly, then shred the meat from the bones (discard the skin). (You should have about 3 cups.)

Remove the chile from its soaking water and finely chop. In a small pot, heat the oil over medium heat. Add the sliced onion, season with salt, and cook, stirring occasionally, until well softened, about 10 minutes. Stir in the chopped garlic and cook for 1 minute more. Add ½ of the chopped chile to the pot with the onion and garlic (you can add more later to taste). Add the tomatoes and increase the heat to bring the tomatoes to a boil. Lower to a simmer and let cook until the liquid has reduced slightly, about 20 minutes. Stir in the epazote and the shredded chicken, and heat until the chicken is warmed through. Taste and adjust the salt or the amount of chile. (This mixture can be stored up to overnight, then reheated in a pot just before proceeding.)

When ready to serve the tostadas, quickly warm up the refried beans in a small pot, thinning them as needed with water to achieve a spreadable consistency. Carefully spread some of the beans onto each warm tostata shell. Top with some of the chicken mixture. Garnish with crema and queso fresco and serve immediately.

Another dish from Mexico's Yucatán region in the south, panuchos are fresh corn tortillas stuffed with pureed or refried black beans, then griddled or deep-fried until lightly crisp. We top our house panuchos with a citrus-and-achiote-marinated chicken, pickled red onions, and a spicy Habanero salsa, all of which are similar to the traditional version.

You can serve one panucho as a snack, or two or three as a meal.

PANUCHOS DE POLLO

Black Bean–Stuffed Tortillas with Shredded Chicken ◦ Makes 8

1 cup cooked black beans plus ¼ cup of their cooking liquid (page 126)

½ teaspoon dried oregano

1 whole (3- to 4-pound) chicken

½ cup Recado Rojo (page 92)

1 cup canned diced tomatoes and their juices

¼ cup freshly squeezed lime juice (from about 3 limes)

½ cup freshly squeezed orange juice (from 1 to 2 oranges)

2 tablespoons kosher salt, plus more to taste

1½ cups Homemade Masa (page 12) or masa prepared from store-bought masa harina

Rice bran oil or canola oil

For serving

2 tablespoons Habanero Salsa (page 221)

1 cup Escabeche Rojo (page 39)

Shaved iceberg lettuce

Add the black beans and their liquid to a food processor with the oregano; puree until smooth. Set aside.

Place the chicken in a large pot or Dutch oven. Add the recado rojo, the tomatoes and their juices, lime juice, orange juice, salt, and enough water to just cover the chicken. Bring to a boil over high heat, then reduce to a simmer. Let cook for 45 minutes.

Remove the chicken (reserve the liquid) and let rest until cool enough to handle. Discard the skin and pick the meat from the bones; discard the bones.

Meanwhile, bring the chicken cooking liquid back to a boil and cook until reduced by half. Transfer the liquid to a blender and blend until smooth. Add back to the pot, then add the chicken. The dish can be prepared to this point one day ahead, cooled fully, then stored in the refrigerator.

To form the panuchos, divide the masa into 8 balls and flatten them slightly with your hand. Line both sides of a tortilla press with a round of plastic cut from a plastic bag. One at a time, place a ball of masa at the center and close the press without pushing down all the way to form a disk slightly thicker than a tortilla (between ⅛ and ¼ inch thick, and about 4 inches wide). Repeat with the remaining balls of masa.

In a large skillet or griddle over medium heat, cook the panuchos, turning once, until just set, about 2 minutes per side. Continue cooking and flipping occasionally until the panucho begins to fill with air, about 2 minutes more. Remove and let cool slightly. Using a paring knife, pierce the rim of each panucho horizontally, then carefully wiggle the knife between the layers, separating them and creating an opening in the top third for filling (it should look like a coin purse).

When ready to serve, fill each panucho evenly with about ¼ cup of the beans.

In a large skillet or griddle over medium-high heat, drizzle in 1 to 2 teaspoons of oil for each panucho; cook, turning once or twice, until lightly crispy on both sides, about 4 minutes total.

Place the panuchos on four individual plates and top with some of the chicken, the salsa, pickled onions, and lettuce.

In Mexico, rice is saved from blandness by the addition of lots of toasted tomato paste—a classic ingredient in almost every version—and, in this recipe, softened onions, carrots, and garlic. Sautéing the uncooked rice in oil for 10 or 15 minutes also brings out the toasty notes before any flavoring is even added. The aromatic, versatile results go well with many small plates and large plates alike, from enchiladas to moles, and of course with beans.

ARROZ MEXICANO

Mexican Rice ○ Serves 6 to 8

¼ cup rice bran oil or canola oil

2 cups basmati rice

¾ cup finely chopped white onion

¾ cup finely diced carrot

1 teaspoon chopped fresh garlic

½ cup tomato paste

3 cups water

2 teaspoons kosher salt, plus more as needed

In a medium pot, heat the oil over medium heat. Add the rice and cook, stirring almost constantly, until the grains start to turn golden and feel lighter and less sticky, 5 to 10 minutes. Add the onions, carrots, and garlic and cook, stirring frequently, until translucent, about 5 minutes. Add the tomato paste and cook, stirring constantly, until it is well incorporated into the rice. Stir in the water and salt. Bring to a boil, then reduce to a simmer. Cook, stirring every 2 to 4 minutes, until the rice looks thickened and starchy, almost like risotto, about 10 minutes. Cover the pot and turn the heat down to very low; let cook without stirring until the rice is tender and all the water is absorbed, 15 to 20 minutes. Taste and season with more salt if needed.

In Spanish, *de la olla* means "cooked in a clay pot," which is how dried beans were traditionally prepared in Mexico. The old grandmas used to say that everything cooked in a clay pot would taste better, but to me, the real secret is using the best-quality beans you can find. Our favorite type is Rancho Gordo pinquito beans, which are slightly smaller than pinto beans and come out creamy and not mushy.

FRIJOLES PINQUITOS DE LA OLLA

Braised Pinquito Beans ○ Makes about 6 cups

2 cups dried pinquito beans (preferably Rancho Gordo brand) or pinto beans

8 cups water

1 tablespoon kosher salt, or more as needed

1 large dried guajillo chile, stemmed and seeded

¼ white onion, sliced through the root

In a large pot, Mexican olla, or Dutch oven, add the beans, water, salt, chile, and onion slices. Bring to a boil over high heat, then reduce to a low simmer. Cover and let cook until the beans are tender and creamy but not falling apart, about 1½ hours. (Alternatively, you can simmer the beans covered in a 350°F oven for 2½ hours.) Taste and adjust the seasoning as needed. Serve immediately or refrigerate overnight and reheat before serving.

Chances are you've had this slightly more indulgent cousin to boiled beans out of a can, but making them yourself produces a richer, creamier, and far more flavorful result—one you will want to eat with breakfast, lunch, and dinner. Refried beans are also great for spreading on taco or tostada shells as a flavor booster and binder for the other toppings.

For the lightest results, fry just what you need for the meal at hand, since reheating them for a second time usually requires adding more oil.

FRIJOLES PINQUITOS REFRITOS

Refried Pinquito Beans ◦ Makes 6 cups

1 cup rice bran oil or canola oil

⅓ white onion, roughly chopped

6 cups Frijoles Pinquitos de la Olla (page 125) or canned pinto beans, drained of half their liquid and warmed (if using with the Huaraches on page 114, drain all the liquid)

1½ teaspoons dried oregano

In a medium pot over medium-high heat, heat the oil until smoking hot. Add the onion and cook, stirring occasionally, until dark golden brown, 3 to 5 minutes. Immediately stir in the warmed beans and oregano to stop the onions from burning. Let cook for 1 to 2 minutes for the flavors to blend and the beans to get hot.

Transfer the bean mixture to a food processor and puree until smooth, adding a little warm water if needed to achieve the desired consistency.

Beans are a universal Mexican side dish, and braising them with a few thoughtful ingredients makes them far more enticing than plain old boiled beans. I infuse the cooking liquid with onion and chile, which give the beans an earthy taste, and I also add a good amount of salt. These are delicious on their own or as a side dish, with some salty, crumbled queso fresco or shredded Jack cheese on top.

FRIJOLES NEGROS DE LA OLLA

Braised Black Beans ◦ Makes 6 cups

2 tablespoons rice bran oil or canola oil

½ white onion, chopped

1 small jalapeño, chopped

2 tablespoons apple cider vinegar

Scant 3 cups dried black beans (16 ounces; preferably Rancho Gordo brand's Midnight Black Beans)

8 cups water

1 tablespoon kosher salt

In a large pot, heat the oil over medium-high heat. Add the onion and jalapeño, lower the heat to medium, and cook, stirring occasionally, until the onion is translucent, about 5 minutes. Pour in the vinegar and let cook until half of it is evaporated, 1 to 2 minutes. Add the beans, water, and salt; bring to a boil over high heat, then reduce the heat to a low simmer. Cover and let cook until the beans are tender and creamy but not falling apart, about 1½ hours. (Alternatively, you can simmer the beans covered in a 350°F oven for 2½ hours.) Taste and adjust the seasoning as needed.

As opposed to refried pinquito beans, which I love to have a creamy, smooth consistency, to me refried black beans are most interesting when they have a bit of a chunkier texture. Believe it or not, there is a specific tool in Mexican cooking called a bean smasher that most Mexican cooks will use. But you can use any other tool that will do the job—like a potato masher or even a large serving fork.

1 cup rice bran oil or canola oil

⅓ white onion, finely chopped

6 cups Frijoles Negros de la Olla (facing page) or canned black beans, drained of all but about 3 cups of their liquid and warmed

1½ teaspoons dried oregano

FRIJOLES NEGROS REFRITOS

Refried Black Beans ○ Makes 6 cups

In a medium pot over medium-high heat, heat the oil until smoking hot. Add the onion and cook, stirring occasionally, until dark golden brown, 3 to 5 minutes. Stir in the warmed beans and the oregano and let cook for 1 to 2 minutes for the flavors to blend and the beans to get hot.

Smash the bean mixture until slightly chunky, adding a little water if needed to reach the desired consistency.

Kosher salt

3 cups diced broccoli florets

2 cups peeled and diced carrots

2 cups diced white onions

2 cups peeled, seeded, and cubed butternut squash

3 cups skin-on cubed potatoes

4 tablespoons Cascabel Chile Oil (recipe follows), or more as needed

Cascabel Chile Oil

6 dried cascabel chiles, stemmed and seeded

1 dried guajillo chile, stemmed and seeded

1½ cups rice bran oil or canola oil

1 small clove garlic, peeled

Doused in a lightly spicy chile oil, sweet, crispy vegetables make a great vegetarian filling for tacos, or work well any time you want a vegetable side dish for antojitos. You can use any combination of vegetables in any proportion you like—sweet potatoes, asparagus, and Brussels sprouts are some good options to throw into the mix.

VEGETALES CON ACEITE DE CHILE CASCABEL

Roasted Vegetables in Cascabel Chile Oil ◦ Serves 6

Preheat the oven to 400°F. Meanwhile, bring a medium pot of water to a boil, and season generously with salt (it should taste like the sea). Set a bowl of ice water next to the stove and season that with salt as well. Add the broccoli to the boiling water and cook until bright green and slightly tenderized, 2 to 3 minutes. Remove with a slotted spoon and transfer to the ice bath to cool; remove and let dry.

In a large bowl, mix the carrots, onions, squash, and potatoes with all but 1 tablespoon of the cascabel oil, and season generously with salt. Spread the vegetables onto two large baking sheets and roast in the oven for 10 minutes. Remove and stir.

Toss the reserved broccoli with the remaining tablespoon of the chile oil, then add the broccoli to the baking sheets. Return to the oven (rotate the location of the pans for more even cooking) and cook until the vegetables are al dente and lightly browned, 10 to 20 minutes more. Taste and adjust the seasoning as necessary.

Cascabel Chile Oil

Makes about 2 cups

Preheat the oven to 350°F. Meanwhile, bring a small pot of water to a boil.

Place the cascabel and guajillo chiles on a baking sheet and roast until the guajillos darken, about 2 minutes; remove from, but do not turn off the oven.

Transfer the chiles to a medium heatproof bowl and cover with the boiling water; let sit until the chiles are soft, about 20 minutes.

Drain the chiles and add them to a blender, along with the oil and garlic; blend thoroughly, until you see a clear red oil. It will keep for up to a few weeks refrigerated in an airtight container.

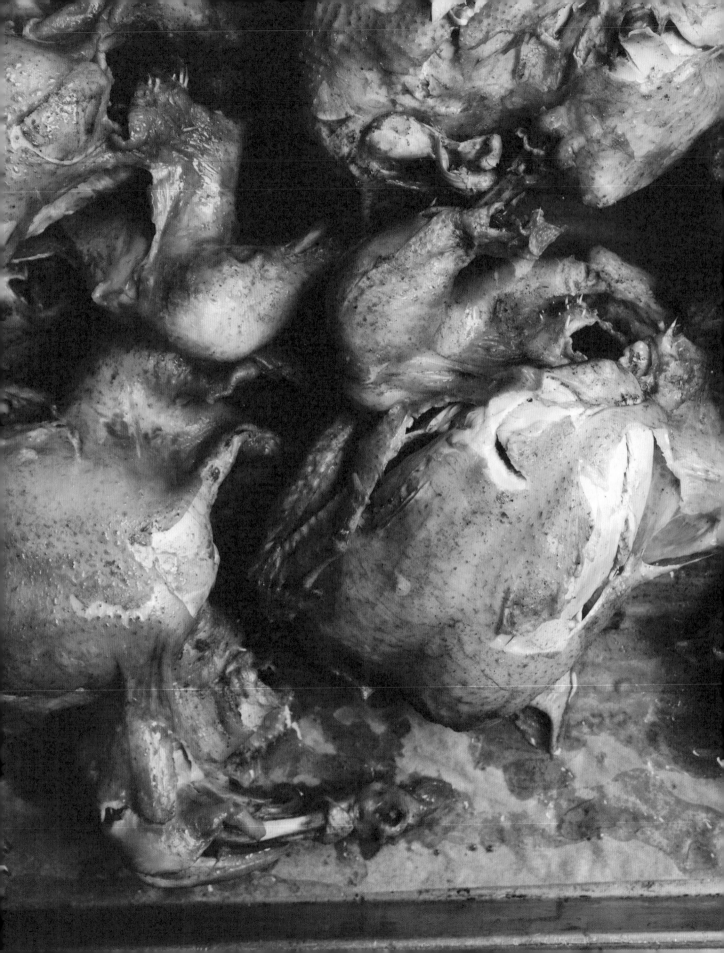

Platillos Fuertes
(BIG PLATES)

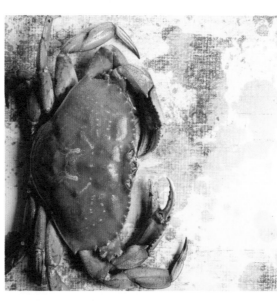

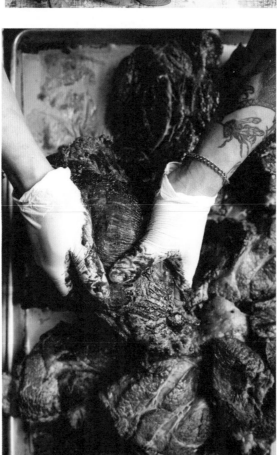

LARGE-BATCH COOKING IS ONE OF THE GREAT PLEASURES OF MEXICAN CUISINE.

During the weekdays, most home cooks in Mexico keep their meals simple, drawing on ingredients like corn masa, eggs, homegrown vegetables, beans, and other inexpensive foods to prepare family lunches and dinners at home. But on weekends or special occasions, at least during my childhood, it seemed as if everyone was out feasting and socializing, as the streets came alive with people eating big platters of food in communal settings.

Historically, many meats were relatively scarce and expensive in Mexico, so items like pork and beef were largely considered special-occasion foods. On Saturdays in my village, local farmers would slaughter an animal and sell it to the townspeople, who would get together and cook it for groups in the community. Oftentimes meats were slow-braised, like carnitas, which included almost the whole pig braised in a gigantic copper pot over a wood fire. To produce the velvety-smooth local moles, sometimes it seemed like a dozen old women were hunched over different worktables toasting a rainbow of chiles, charring tortillas, and grinding aromatic spices to make enough to feed dozens. Everyone had a job, and there was nothing like the moment dinner was ready and all of us, kids and adults, could heap our plates high with the fruits of the day's labor.

This section is full of these larger main-course dishes, many of which are meant to be slow-cooked in big batches and eaten family-style. In putting this book together, I couldn't bear to shortcut these recipes so that they would *always* fit into the quick-and-easy category, so many of them include the original steps I remember my mama and the other village women following at home. Of course, you and I can achieve the same cooking and prepping tasks more quickly and easily thanks to the modern conveniences of high-powered blenders, gas or electric stoves, and food processors. But as you will see, creating everything from scratch is the true secret to re-creating the complex flavors and colors of true Mexican cuisine. You can break down the longer recipe steps over the course of a day, or a weekend, or even a week. Many of the components can be quickly and easily made ahead, and frozen or reserved in the fridge until serving time.

Several of the *platillos fuertes*, or large plates, in this section come with suggested side dishes and accompaniments. There is no need for rigid formality in how you eat or serve the dishes you make; feel free to skip forks altogether and use tortillas to scoop up the saucy meats and vegetables and spoon them into your mouth—a quintessential part of enjoying Mexican home cooking.

Chilaquiles is one of the most common breakfasts in Mexico, popular in home cooking because of its ease and heartiness, and also for being a great hangover cure. The point is to use up tortillas from the day before, cutting them into shapes and sautéing them with green or red salsa, spices or aromatics, and scrambled eggs. But chilaquiles can also be eaten later in the day, when you can substitute chicken, beef, or chorizo for the eggs. I add a drizzle of crema to balance the acidity from the salsa, and garnish with queso fresco, sliced green onion, and fresh cilantro.

CHILAQUILES ROJOS CON HUEVOS

Red Chilaquiles with Scrambled Eggs ○ Serves 6

To make the salsa, heat a large skillet or griddle to high heat and add all of the dried chiles; cook, rotating frequently with tongs, until blistered in places but not burnt, 1 to 2 minutes total. Transfer the chiles to a heatproof bowl and cover with boiling water; let sit until softened, about 20 minutes.

Remove the chiles from their soaking water and transfer to a blender along with the tomatoes, garlic, and a generous pinch of salt; puree the salsa until smooth.

Heat the ¼ cup oil in a large pot over medium-high heat. Pour the salsa into the pot quickly and all at once (be careful, as the oil may splatter), and bring the salsa to a boil. Stir in the water, bring to a simmer, and let cook for 20 minutes. Taste and add more salt as necessary. (Salsa can be prepared a day in advance.)

When ready to serve, fry the tortillas: Set a paper towel–lined platter next to the stove. In a large skillet, preheat the 2 cups oil until very hot, then add half of the tortilla pieces. Cook, stirring with tongs to flip and submerge the tortillas as needed, until very crispy, 6 to 10 minutes. Remove using a slotted spoon or tongs and transfer to the prepared plate. Repeat with the remaining tortillas.

Transfer ¼ cup of the frying oil (or use fresh oil if desired) to a large nonstick skillet. Heat the oil over medium-high heat and add the onions; lower the heat to medium and cook, stirring occasionally, until translucent, about 5 minutes. Pour in the beaten eggs all at once. When the layer of eggs looks about halfway cooked, distribute the fried tortilla pieces in the pan, allowing the eggs to stick to the chips. Cook, stirring constantly to scramble and distribute the eggs among the tortillas, until the eggs are cooked through. Add the salsa and mix well to coat.

To serve, transfer the chilaquiles to a large serving plate and top with the crema, queso fresco, cilantro, and green onions.

Salsa

5 dried guajillo chiles, stemmed and seeded

2 dried ancho chiles, stemmed and seeded

2 dried morita chiles, stemmed

2 dried chipotle chiles, stemmed and seeded

⅔ cup (5 ounces) canned diced tomatoes with their juices

2 cloves garlic

Salt

¼ cup rice bran oil or canola oil

3 cups water

Chilaquiles

2 cups rice bran oil or canola oil

12 soft corn tortillas, cut into 1-inch squares (4 cups)

½ cup chopped white onion

6 eggs, beaten

For serving

½ cup Crema (page 35) or sour cream

½ cup crumbled queso fresco

Chopped fresh cilantro leaves

Thinly sliced green onions

This dish was inspired by the north of Mexico, where a thicker tortilla is commonly used as a base on which to build breakfast (the name translates as "eggs in a box"). The poached eggs are not a traditional element (in Mexican home kitchens, eggs are almost always served scrambled), but at Nopalito we love how their runny yolk blends with the salsa and refried beans to further flavor the dish.

HUEVOS DE CAJA

Serves 2

2 tablespoons rice bran oil or canola oil

2 homemade soft corn tortillas (see page 16) or store-bought soft corn tortillas

1 tablespoon kosher salt

1 tablespoon white vinegar or freshly squeezed lemon juice

4 eggs

1 cup (8 ounces) Frijoles Negros Refritos (page 127) or good-quality store-bought refried beans, warmed

¼ cup plus 2 tablespoons Salsa Cilantro (page 218)

¾ cup grated Jack cheese

Chopped cilantro leaves

Preheat the oven to 350°F. In a medium pot, bring 4 cups water to a boil.

Meanwhile, set a paper towel–lined plate next to the stove. In a large skillet or griddle, heat the oil over medium-high heat until very hot. Add the tortillas and cook, turning occasionally, until crispy on both sides, about 6 minutes. Transfer to the prepared plate to drain some of the oil.

Season the boiling water with the salt and pour in the vinegar. Lower the heat to a steady simmer. One at a time, crack the eggs into a small bowl, and carefully ease them into the water. Cook until the outsides are set and the insides are still runny, 3 to 4 minutes. Remove using a slotted spoon, and set aside.

Place the tortillas in two small round individual-sized cazuelas, cast-iron skillets, or similar baking dishes. Divide the warm refried beans among the tortillas, forming a circular "nest" shape in the center of each (if needed, you can thin the beans with a little water before adding). Place two poached eggs atop each bean pile, and divide the salsa among the portions, pouring it on top. Sprinkle with the Jack cheese and bake in the oven until the cheese is completely melted, about 5 minutes. Serve immediately, garnished with cilantro.

Puerco is Spanish for "pork," and this comforting bean dish is named after the pork traditionally used in the braise. It's from the north of Mexico, where the weather is not as tropical and therefore much of the land is used to raise animals like pigs and cattle rather than to grow hot-weather fruits and vegetables. You can use any kind of pork, but we like bacon and chorizo for the added smokiness they lend to the beans.

In Mexico, bean dishes are served alongside meats like carne asada or carnitas. But at the restaurant we add eggs to turn these beans into a brunch or lunch entree. Be sure to cook the eggs fully before you add the beans; otherwise, they will emulsify into the bean liquid, dulling the color and turning it cloudy.

FRIJOLES PUERCOS CON HUEVOS

Pork-Braised Butter Beans with Scrambled Eggs ○ Serves 4

In a large pot or Dutch oven, combine the beans, 3 cups water, and the salt. Wrap the onion, garlic, epazote, and guajillo chile (if using) tightly in a piece of cheesecloth and add it to the pot with the beans; bring to a boil, then reduce to a simmer. Place a parchment paper round atop the liquid in the pot, or partially cover the pot with a lid, and let cook until the beans are fully tender, 1½ to 2 hours. (At this point you can cool and store the beans and their liquid until ready to assemble the dish.)

In a large pot or high-sided skillet, heat the oil over medium heat. Add the bacon and cook, stirring occasionally, until some of the fat has been rendered and the meat is browned. Add the chorizo and cook, stirring often and breaking up the meat as you cook, until the meat is heated through, about 5 minutes.

Quickly whisk the eggs in a medium bowl, then pour them into the chorizo mixture and cook, stirring occasionally, until the eggs are just set and no longer runny. Stir in the beans and their liquid, making sure there is enough liquid to cover all of the ingredients (if not, add a little more water). Bring to a boil, then reduce to a simmer; let cook for 5 minutes for the flavors to blend.

To serve, divide among four serving bowls. Garnish with salsa escabeche, the queso fresco, cilantro, and green onions.

Pork-Braised Butter Beans

1 cup dried butter beans

1 tablespoon kosher salt, plus more as needed

½ white onion

3 cloves garlic

5 fresh epazote, basil, or cilantro leaves

1 dried guajillo chile (optional)

¼ cup rice bran oil or canola oil

1 cup diced bacon

12 ounces Chorizo Oaxaqueño (page 44) or store-bought Mexican chorizo, casings removed

Eggs and serving

8 eggs

Salsa Escabeche (page 228; optional)

Crumbled queso fresco

Chopped fresh cilantro

Thinly sliced green onion

Machaca means "mash" in Spanish, and that is precisely what you do with the shrimp in this recipe, mashing and mixing small pieces of it with softened onions, garlic, and jalapeño. In addition to serving machaca with eggs for brunch, we also use this shrimp mixture to fill crispy fried Empanadas de Camarón (page 110).

The salsa ligera—a mixture of tomatoes with a lot of cumin, chiles, and aromatics—is not used purely to spice up the dish the way some salsas are; it's more of a savory, stew-like sauce that's intended to coat and moisten all of the other ingredients. Green onions and fresh cilantro brighten up the dish at the end and are great with the fresh seafood.

MACHACA DE CAMARÓN CON HUEVOS

Smashed Shrimp with Eggs and Salsa   ○   Serves 4

To make the salsa, in a blender, puree the tomatoes, onion, jalapeños, garlic, cumin, peppercorns, and a pinch of salt until very smooth.

In a large skillet or pot, heat the 2 tablespoons oil over medium-high heat. Add the salsa all at once (be careful, as the oil may splatter slightly) and bring to a boil; reduce to a simmer and let cook for 15 minutes. Taste and adjust the seasoning as needed. Turn off the heat but keep warm.

To make the machaca, in a separate medium pot, heat the ¼ cup oil over medium-high heat. Add the onions, garlic, and jalapeño and season with salt; cook until the vegetables are softened, being sure the garlic doesn't brown too deeply, about 5 minutes, then add the tomatoes. Bring to a boil, then reduce to a simmer and let cook for 10 minutes. Add the shrimp and smash it into small pieces using the tip of a wooden spoon. As soon as the shrimp has turned pink and opaque, about 5 minutes, turn off the heat.

Beat the eggs in a medium bowl and season with salt. In a large skillet over medium heat, heat the ¼ cup oil until warmed through, then add the eggs and cook, stirring to scramble, until just set and no longer runny. Stir the shrimp mixture into the eggs.

Divide the machaca among four serving bowls. Top each with ¾ cup of the salsa ligera, and garnish with the cilantro and green onions. Serve with warm tortillas and refried black beans if desired.

Salsa Ligera

4 cups (32 ounces) canned diced tomatoes and their juices

¼ white onion, roughly chopped (about ¼ cup)

2 to 3 jalapeños, stemmed

5 cloves garlic

1½ teaspoons ground cumin

¼ teaspoon whole black peppercorns

Salt

2 tablespoons rice bran oil or canola oil

Shrimp Machaca

¼ cup rice bran oil or canola oil

1 white onion, diced (about 1 cup)

2 cloves garlic, chopped

1 jalapeño, diced

2 cups (16 ounces) canned diced tomatoes and their juices

Salt

1 pound fresh shrimp, peeled and cleaned

Eggs and serving

8 eggs

Salt

¼ cup rice bran oil or canola oil

Chopped fresh cilantro

Julienned green onions

8 to 12 warm soft corn tortillas (optional)

Frijoles Negros Refritos (page 127) or store-bought refried black beans (optional)

With a rich, nearly black color and earthy flavor, this traditional stew gets many of its signature qualities from the toasted dried pasilla chiles and chiles negros blended into the broth. To balance the deep flavors with some acidity and freshness, and to add body and another layer of spice, we blend in fresh tomatillos, serrano chiles, and jalapeños.

It is best to leave the fat on the beef shoulder unless it is really excessive, since the fat will flavor the stew as it cooks, but you can always skim it off the top of the pot at the end if you prefer a leaner result. To eat, use the warm tortillas to pick up pieces of the stewed meat with your fingers and spoon them into your mouth.

10 medium tomatillos, husked and rinsed

2 serrano chiles

3 jalapeños

6 cloves garlic

5 dried mulato chiles, stemmed and seeded

8 dried pasilla chiles, stemmed and seeded

5 dried chiles negros, stemmed and seeded

Kosher salt

2 pounds trimmed beef shoulder, diced into 1-inch cubes

¼ cup rice bran oil or canola oil

For serving

Warm soft corn tortillas

Cooked white rice (optional)

GUISADO DE RES DE PASILLA

Stewed Beef with Pasilla Chiles   o   Serves 6

Preheat the oven to 350°F. In a roasting pan, combine the tomatillos, serranos, jalapeños, garlic, and 2 cups water; roast for 30 minutes. Remove the pan and set aside; lower the heat to 325°F.

Meanwhile, preheat a large skillet or griddle over medium-high heat; add all of the dried chiles, working in batches as needed, and toast, rotating them every 10 seconds or so with tongs, until intensified in color and charred in places, about 1 minute total. Transfer to a heatproof bowl and cover with boiling water; let sit until softened, about 20 minutes.

In a blender, combine the softened chiles (reserve the soaking water), 2 or 3 of the roasted tomatillos, and ½ teaspoon salt; puree into a smooth, thick paste, adding a little of the soaking water as needed to blend. Working in batches as needed, add the remaining tomatillos, serranos, jalapeños, and the liquid from the roasting pan and blend just until chunky in texture.

Season the beef all over with ½ teaspoon salt. In a large pot or Dutch oven over high heat, heat the oil until hot but not smoking. Working in three batches, add the meat and brown, turning occasionally, until golden brown on all sides, about 10 minutes. Pour in the chile-tomatillo mixture and stir to combine. Cover the pot, transfer to the oven, and braise until the meat is very tender, about 2 hours. Taste and adjust the seasoning as needed. Serve with warm tortillas and white rice if desired.

The ultimate dish to serve on a cold day, this soup is made with a consommé, a rich, fortified stock that is simmered for a long time to deepen its flavor, then strained so it comes out clear (not murky). The soup is both chunky and brothy, with moist, shredded chicken, chickpeas, and diced vegetables. The bowls are lined with big chunks of queso fresco and avocado before the soup is ladled in, making it even heartier and more comforting. Finally, a chipotle chile floats on top—and the more of the chile you stir and mash into your bowl, the spicier and smokier your soup will be.

Feel free to change the vegetables with the seasons, but the constant elements should be the slow-cooked stock; fresh chunks of avocado; chickpeas (or substitute rice) for starchiness; and the soft, silky lumps of queso fresco.

CALDO TLALPEÑO CON POLLO

Clear Chicken and Vegetable Soup from Tlalpeño   ○   Serves 6

1 small (3-pound) chicken, cut into 6 pieces, or 2 each bone-in, skin-on breasts, thighs, and legs

½ white onion

4 cloves garlic

2 bay leaves

1 teaspoon whole black peppercorns

Kosher salt

1 cup finely diced peeled butternut squash (½-inch cubes)

1 cup finely diced peeled carrots (from about 2 carrots)

1 cup diced cauliflower florets

1 cup diced broccoli florets

1 (15-ounce) can cooked chickpeas, drained and rinsed

For serving

8 ounces queso fresco, cut into 1-inch cubes

1½ firm-ripe avocados, diced

3 Chipotles Adobados (page 42) or 3 canned chipotle chiles in adobo

Fresh cilantro leaves

Julienned green onions

1 lime, cut into 6 wedges

12 warm soft corn tortillas (optional)

To make the consommé, in a large stockpot, combine the chicken, 6 quarts water, the onion, garlic, bay leaves, and peppercorns; bring to a boil, then immediately reduce to a simmer. Skim any foam and fat that rise to the top and discard. Let cook for 45 minutes, then skim the stock again. Remove the chicken and let cool slightly, then pull all the meat off the bones and discard the skin (you will have about 4 cups meat). Place the bones back in the pot, add 1 teaspoon salt, and continue cooking at a very low simmer for about 2 hours. Strain with a fine-mesh strainer and adjust the seasoning as needed. (At this point you can cool and refrigerate the stock for up to 1 week until ready to serve.)

Bring a medium pot of water to a boil and season generously with salt. Set a large bowl of ice water next to the stove and season it with salt as well. Add the butternut squash to the boiling water and let cook until softened but still al dente, 3 to 4 minutes. Remove using a slotted spoon and transfer to the ice water to cool. Add the carrots to the boiling water and let cook until al dente, 2 to 3 minutes; transfer to the ice bath. Add the broccoli and cauliflower and let cook until al dente, 40 seconds to 1 minute; transfer to the ice bath; once they have cooled, drain.

When ready to serve the soup, skim off any fat that has risen to the top of the stock. Bring the consommé back to a boil. Add the chicken meat, vegetables, and chickpeas and cook until heated through and the vegetables are to your desired doneness.

Divide the queso fresco and avocado among six large soup bowls. Ladle the soup into the bowls. Cut the chiles in half lengthwise and place half atop each bowl, then sprinkle with the cilantro and green onions. Serve each bowl with a wedge of lime for squeezing and 2 warm tortillas for dunking, if desired.

Pozole is one of Mexico's oldest soups, supposedly dating back to Aztec times. Though nowadays there are a million different versions, this old-school recipe has a smoky red stock spiced with pureed chiles. You wouldn't call it pozole without the addition of hominy—whole white corn kernels that have been acidified to soften their casings and render their kernels plump and chewy.

Pozole is all about the garnishes, from corn chips to radishes, limes, cabbage, and fresh oregano. Feel free to pile them high in your bowl. And because every Mexican has to have something spicy on the table, we finish ours with a mix of ground chili powders (or you can substitute hot sauce).

You need a large stockpot to make this dish, or you can divide it among two large (6-quart) Dutch ovens.

POZOLE ROJO

Red Pork Soup with Hominy　○　Serves 6 to 8

½ yellow onion

2 cloves garlic

8 stems cilantro, plus fresh cilantro leaves for serving (optional)

2 bay leaves

4 pounds pork shoulder, trimmed and cut into 1-inch cubes

Kosher salt

Adobo (recipe follows)

8 cups cooked hominy (page 43) or store-bought canned hominy

For serving

4 cups julienned green cabbage (about 1 small-to-medium head)

16 breakfast radishes, thinly sliced

½ medium red onion, thinly sliced

4 limes, halved

2 tablespoons Nopalito Spices (page 35; optional) or store-bought chili powder

Chopped fresh oregano, or dried

4 cups tortilla chips

In a piece of cheesecloth, wrap the yellow onion, garlic, cilantro stems, and bay leaves; secure with twine to form a bundle, then set aside.

Season the pork on all sides generously with salt. Place the pork, adobo, and the cheesecloth sachet in a large stockpot; add 6 quarts water to cover, and stir or whisk to incorporate the adobo. Season generously with salt, then bring to a boil. Reduce to a simmer and let cook until the pork is tender, about 1 hour.

In a blender, puree 1 cup of the hominy with about 1 cup of the braising liquid from the pork. Add the pureed hominy and the remaining 7 cups hominy to the pozole and bring back to a boil. Turn off the heat and let cool slightly, then skim away the excess fat that rises to the top. (Pozole can be made in advance and refrigerated at this stage.)

Bring the stew back to a simmer. Taste and adjust the seasoning as needed. Ladle into 6 to 8 serving bowls and serve with the cabbage, radishes, red onion, limes, Nopalito spices, oregano, cilantro, and tortilla chips.

Adobo

8 large dried ancho chiles, stemmed and seeded

2 cloves garlic

1 large white onion, roughly chopped

1½ teaspoons dried Mexican oregano

1 teaspoon cumin seeds

Salt

Adobo

Place the chiles in a heatproof bowl and add boiling water to cover; let sit until the chiles are softened, about 20 minutes.

Transfer the chiles to a blender (reserve the soaking water). Add the garlic, onion, oregano, cumin, and a generous pinch of salt to the blender and puree, adding just enough of the soaking water to form a thick, smooth paste.

This is one of the most nostalgic recipes from my childhood, a brothy chicken noodle soup that my mom would make on gloomy days. Because my hometown of Veracruz was once occupied by the Spanish, their use of saffron became ingrained in our regional cuisine. It gives the soup a vibrant orange-red tinge. The Spanish also brought *fideos*, skinny dried wheat noodles similar to angel hair, which we would fry and add to soups to give them color and a deep toasty flavor. You can find fideos at any Mexican market or online, or use dried angel hair pasta.

While frying the fideos, reserve a few extras off to the side to salt and eat while they are still crispy and hot. They are an addictive snack, and when I was a kid in Mexico, these were one of my favorite foods.

SOPA DE POLLO CON FIDEOS

Chicken Soup with Fried Noodles ○ Serves 4

Season the chicken with salt. Place in a large stockpot and pour in 3 quarts water to cover; season the water generously with salt. Bring to a boil, then reduce to a simmer; let cook for 30 minutes.

Meanwhile, set a paper towel–lined plate next to the stove. In a large skillet, heat the oil until it registers 350°F on a deep-fat thermometer, then add the fideos. Fry until golden brown and crunchy, 1 to 2 minutes. Remove using a slotted spoon or tongs and transfer to the prepared plate.

In a blender, puree the tomato paste, saffron, garlic, onions, and 1 cup water. Add to the pot with the chicken and continue cooking for another 20 minutes. Add the carrots and cook for 5 minutes. Add the fideos and cook for 5 minutes more. Taste and adjust the seasoning of the soup as needed.

Ladle into 4 serving bowls and garnish with the cilantro, jalapeño, and onions. Serve with warm tortillas if desired.

Soup

½ (3- to 4-pound) chicken, cut into 4 pieces

Salt

1 cup rice bran oil or canola oil

½ pound fideos or dried angel hair pasta, broken into 5-inch-long pieces

½ cup tomato paste

½ teaspoon loosely packed saffron

2 cloves garlic

½ cup diced white onion (from about ½ medium onion)

1 cup peeled, diced carrots

For serving

Fresh cilantro leaves

Thinly sliced jalapeños

Finely diced white onion

4 to 8 soft corn tortillas, warmed (optional)

Located right along the Gulf of Mexico, Veracruz is the birthplace of this coastal soup, a spiced seafood broth bursting with fresh whole pieces of fish and shellfish and lightly thickened with masa. The word *tesmole* refers to the combination of chiles and other aromatics used to make the broth (you'll notice it's similar to mole, a dish that blends many chiles, herbs, and spices), so the base is a bit like a combination of a mole and broth. Be sure to make the adobo before starting on the soup—perhaps while you simmer the stock.

You can change the seafood according to whatever looks good at the market, but be sure to include the crab and shrimp. Their shells, which you should reserve when harvesting the meat, are the secret to the stock's sweet flavor.

TESMOLE DE MARISCOS

Spicy Seafood Soup   ◦   Serves 8

To make the stock, in a medium pot, combine the crab and shrimp shells, the onion, garlic, bay leaf, peppercorns, salt, and water. Bring to a boil, then reduce to a simmer and let cook for 30 minutes. Strain and discard the shells and aromatics. (At this point you can cool and refrigerate the stock for up to 3 days, or freeze for up to 1 month until ready to proceed.)

To make the soup, in a large pot or Dutch oven, heat the oil over medium heat. Add the onions and garlic and season with salt; cook, stirring occasionally, until the onions are soft and translucent (do not brown), 10 to 15 minutes. Stir in the adobo and cook, stirring occasionally, for another 10 minutes; then stir in the homemade stock and ½ teaspoon salt. Bring to a boil, then reduce to a simmer and let cook for 30 minutes. Taste and adjust the salt as needed.

In a medium bowl, whisk the masa with ¼ cup water. Slowly whisk the masa mixture into the soup, keeping the heat high enough and adding the masa slowly enough to maintain a strong simmer. Add the crab meat, shrimp, clams, and mussels, and cover the pot; cook until the clams and mussels open, about 5 minutes. (Discard any that do not open.)

Taste the soup and adjust the seasoning as needed. Ladle the soup into bowls and garnish with cilantro. Serve with the lime wedges and tostadas, tortillas, or chips if desired.

Stock

2 large Dungeness crabs, shells removed and reserved, meat picked (about 2 cups; see page 58)

4 cups fresh raw shrimp (about 2 pounds), cleaned, shells removed and reserved

¼ white onion

2 cloves garlic

1 bay leaf

1½ teaspoons whole black peppercorns

1 teaspoon kosher salt

8 cups water

Soup

¼ cup rice bran oil or canola oil

4 cups sliced white onion (from about 2 onions)

1½ teaspoons chopped fresh garlic

½ teaspoon kosher salt, plus more as needed

Adobo (recipe follows)

¼ cup Homemade Masa (page 12) or masa prepared from store-bought masa harina

¼ cup water

1 pound fresh clams, scrubbed

1 pound fresh mussels, scrubbed

For serving

Fresh cilantro leaves

Lime wedges, for squeezing

Warm tostadas, tortillas, or tortilla chips (optional)

Adobo

3 cups (24 ounces) canned diced tomatoes and their juices

1 clove garlic

8 medium dried chiles de árbol, stemmed and seeded

5 dried guajillo chiles, stemmed and seeded

Kosher salt

Adobo

Preheat the oven to 350°F. Place the tomatoes and garlic in a roasting pan and add 4 cups water. Roast for 1 hour.

Meanwhile, place all of the chiles in a heatproof bowl and cover with boiling water; let soak until softened, about 20 minutes. Transfer to a blender (reserve the soaking water) and puree, adding a little of the soaking water as needed to blend into a thick, smooth paste.

When the roasted tomato and garlic mixture is done, add to the blender with the chile paste. Add a generous pinch of salt and puree until smooth.

Birria is a rich red stew that originated in western Mexico, in the state of Jalisco. Traditionally it was made with lamb or goat, but today, places called *birrerias* serve all kinds of variations on the stew, made with chicken, beef, or other meats. Some chiles and spices just work better with different types of meat (usually dark with dark, light with light), so for our beef stew we make an adobo using dark, earthy, aromatic chiles. Since there are a lot of moving parts to this recipe, you may want to do a few of the steps—such as marinating the beef and making the pickles—a day before. Also, be sure to make the adobo first, since you need it for both the birria and this dish's accompanying salsa.

A good trick is to start searing the short ribs with their fatty sides down so they release their own fats for sautéing. And if you can get your hands on a banana leaf, or better yet an agave leaf, it's worth it—the leaf is the source of much of the dish's earthy flavor.

BIRRIA AL RES

Short Rib Stew ○ Serves 8 to 10

A half day to a full day before you plan to serve, season the short ribs heavily with salt; let sit 30 minutes.

Heat a large pot or Dutch oven over medium-high heat. Brown the meat in a single layer, working in batches as needed to avoid crowding the pot; cook, turning occasionally, until some of the fat is rendered and the meat is golden brown on all sides, then remove to a platter. Once all the ribs are seared, marinate the meat in half of the birria adobo and let it rest in the refrigerator for at least 4 hours or up to overnight.

Preheat the oven to 325°F. Lay the banana leaf across the bottom of a pot or Dutch oven, then place the meat and marinade on top. Cut the onion half into four pieces and arrange the pieces over the meat along with the garlic, bay leaves, and peppercorns. Add enough water to cover the meat by 1 inch. Fold the ends of the banana leaf over the meat to cover. Seal the pan with aluminum foil or a lid and transfer to the oven. Cook until very tender, about 3 hours. Drain the meat, reserving the braising liquid. (If not serving immediately, you can refrigerate the liquid and meat until ready to serve, up to 2 days.)

To make the salsa, raise the oven heat to 350°F. Place the diced tomatoes and garlic on a baking sheet or in a roasting pan and roast for 30 minutes. Remove and let cool slightly.

Birria

8 pounds beef short ribs (about 6 large ribs)

Kosher salt

Birria Adobo (recipe follows), divided

1 large banana leaf or agave leaf (optional)

½ medium white onion

6 cloves garlic

3 bay leaves

1 teaspoon whole black peppercorns

Salsa

8 cups (64 ounces) canned diced tomatoes and their juices

3 cloves garlic

18 dried cascabel chiles, stemmed and seeded

For serving

16 to 20 warm homemade soft corn tortillas (see page 16) or store-bought soft corn tortillas (optional)

Chopped fresh cilantro

Escabeche Rojo (page 39) or diced raw red onions

Hot sauce (optional)

CONTINUED

Birria Adobo

8 cloves garlic

1 tablespoon whole black peppercorns

2 teaspoons whole cloves

1½ teaspoons ground ginger

1 teaspoon ground cumin

1 tablespoon plus 1½ teaspoons dried thyme

1 tablespoon plus 1½ teaspoons dried oregano

7 bay leaves

3 tablespoons sesame seeds

22 dried ancho chiles, stemmed and seeded

1 cup dark Mexican beer, such as Negra Modelo

¼ cup white vinegar

Meanwhile, heat a medium skillet to medium heat and add the cascabel chiles; cook, turning occasionally, until the chiles turn bright red and charred in places, 1 to 2 minutes total. Transfer the chiles, roasted tomatoes and garlic, and the remaining half of the birria adobo to a blender, working in batches if needed, and blend until very smooth.

In a large pot, combine the salsa with half of the braising liquid, or more as needed to achieve a rich but still runny consistency; bring to a boil, then reduce to a simmer and let cook for 30 minutes. Cut the short ribs into large chunks (about 3 inches) and add the meat to the sauce; taste and adjust the salt as necessary.

Serve the birria with warm tortillas, cilantro, pickled onions, and hot sauce, if desired.

Birria Adobo

Makes 4 cups

Preheat the oven to 350°F. On a parchment paper–lined baking sheet, combine the garlic, peppercorns, cloves, ginger, cumin, thyme, oregano, bay leaves, and sesame seeds. Bake until the sesame seeds are lightly browned (but not blackened) and the spices are lightly toasted and aromatic, about 15 minutes.

Meanwhile, in a medium heatproof bowl, cover the chiles with boiling water; let sit until softened, about 20 minutes.

Transfer the spices, chiles (reserve the soaking water), beer, and vinegar to a blender and blend, adding a little of the soaking water as needed to form a smooth, thick paste. The adobo will keep for up to 1 week.

Because in my village, and other smaller villages of Mexico, beef was relatively scarce and expensive, you would rarely, if ever, be served a whole steak. That is why *bisteces à la Mexicana* is traditionally cut into small pieces, perfect for sharing.

As with many large-batch meat dishes in the Mexican culture, this one is meant to be scooped up with tortillas—or, better yet, tortillas filled with a little white rice—and eaten with your fingers.

BISTECES À LA MEXICANA

Mexican-Style Stewed Steak ○ Serves 6

2 pounds top sirloin, trimmed and diced into 1-inch cubes

Kosher salt

¼ cup rice bran oil or canola oil

1 white onion, sliced

4 jalapeños, stemmed and sliced

1 teaspoon dried oregano

1 teaspoon ground cumin

4 red heirloom tomatoes, finely diced (2 cups), or 2 cups canned diced tomatoes and their juices

Leaves from ½ bunch cilantro

For serving

Warm soft corn tortillas

Cooked white rice

Jalapeños Curtidos (page 39) or store-bought pickled jalapeños

Season the meat all over with salt, and let rest for 1 hour.

In a large cast-iron pan over high heat, heat the oil until hot but not smoking. Add the meat and cook, stirring occasionally, until golden brown, 4 to 5 minutes. Stir in the onion, jalapeños, oregano, and cumin, and cook, stirring occasionally, until the vegetables are caramelized, about 10 minutes. Lower the heat, then stir in the tomatoes; cover and cook at a very low simmer, stirring every 5 minutes to prevent sticking, until the meat is tender, about 45 minutes. Add the cilantro.

Divide the meat among 6 plates or serve family-style with warm tortillas, rice, and the pickled jalapeños on the side.

Carne asada is a ubiquitous feature of American taquerias, but we wanted to do something different with our version. In Mexico, it is very popular to combine two types of meat or seafood in one dish—typically a leaner meat with a fattier one—so here we added the rich chorizo to complement the nice lean skirt steak. Adding cooked cactus absorbs some of the chorizo fats as well, lending a vegetable component to an otherwise meaty meal. We serve it with salsa borracha, a chunky, dark chile–based salsa with a little sweetness and a splash of tequila for acidity and kick (*borracha* means "drunk" in Spanish).

Even though this carne asada recipe is an entrée, you can forgo the fork and knife: it is meant to be scooped up with warm tortillas and eaten by hand like we do in Mexico.

½ cup freshly squeezed lime juice (from about 4 limes), plus the zest of 2 limes

½ cup olive oil

2 pounds top sirloin or skirt steak, trimmed

Salt

4 medium nopales (cactus leaves), spines trimmed away

1 cup crumbled Chorizo Oaxaqueño (page 44) or crumbled store-bought Mexican chorizo, casings removed

For serving

Fresh cilantro leaves

Salsa Borracha (page 228)

8 to 12 warm homemade soft corn tortillas (see page 16) or store-bought soft corn tortillas

CARNE ASADA CON CHORIZO

Grilled Steak with Chorizo ○ Serves 4 to 6

In a large bowl, whisk together the lime juice, lime zest, and olive oil. Season the beef well with salt and add it to the citrus mixture; let marinate at room temperature, stirring occasionally, for about 1 hour.

Meanwhile, rinse the cactus leaves with cold water and season with salt. In a large skillet or griddle over high heat, working in batches if needed, cook the cactus leaves until charred on both sides and slightly browned, about 3 minutes per side. Remove and let cool slightly, then slice into ½-inch-wide strips. In the same skillet, lower the heat to medium and add the crumbled chorizo. Cook, stirring occasionally, until warmed through and fully cooked, about 6 minutes. Stir the sliced cactus into the chorizo. Turn off the heat but keep the mixture warm.

When ready to serve, preheat a grill or griddle to high heat. Add the steak and let cook, turning once, until medium, about 3 minutes per side; remove and let rest about 5 minutes.

Slice the steak against the grain into ¼-inch-thick pieces. Transfer to a large platter or divide among 4 to 6 individual plates. Garnish the steak with cilantro and serve with the chorizo and cactus mixture, the salsa borracha, and warm tortillas on the side.

Carnitas is one of those obsessed-about Mexican dishes to which everyone wants to know the secrets. Traditionally it included the whole pig and all of its parts—the ears, the tail, the liver, and tripe—fried in lard in a giant copper pot. Most often the meat was eaten right on the spot, fresh from the vat.

We wanted, the sought-after moist, delicious, golden-brown carnitas with all of the authentic flavor, but we also wanted the flexibility to cook them ahead of time and still be able to serve them later without their drying out. The secret is to sizzle them first in lard, then braise them with a little milk, beer, and piloncillo. The sugar gives a subtle sweetness similar to barbecue. We like to serve ours with cabbage salad for crunch, the tanginess of the lime dressing, and contrast.

If you want more color and crispness when reheating your carnitas, spread the meat out on a pan and bake it at 450°F to caramelize the outside and render the edges shiny and brown.

CARNITAS

Serves 6

5 pounds boneless pork shoulder (pork butt), cut into 3-inch cubes

Kosher salt

¼ orange

½ white onion

3 cloves garlic

1 bay leaf

½ cinnamon stick

4 pounds lard

2 ounces piloncillo or ¼ cup brown sugar

¼ cup whole milk

¼ cup dark Mexican beer, such as Negra Modelo

For serving

Salsa Cruda (page 223)

Ensalada de Repollo (page 179)

Jalapeños Curtidos (page 39; optional)

12 to 18 warm soft corn tortillas

Season the pork generously with salt and refrigerate for 2 hours or up to 24 hours.

In a square of cheesecloth, wrap the orange, onion, garlic, bay leaf, and cinnamon stick, and secure with kitchen twine to form a bundle.

In a large, heavy-bottomed pot, cook the lard over high heat until melted. Add the pork, the piloncillo, and the cheesecloth packet. Bring the lard to a boil, then lower the heat to medium and let cook, stirring every 10 minutes, until the meat turns light golden brown and is almost falling apart, about 90 minutes (lower the heat as needed to prevent the meat from overdarkening or burning, or crank it up for the last 10 minutes as needed to achieve browning). Reduce the heat to low and add the milk and beer (be careful, as the lard may splatter). Cook at a low simmer until the meat starts to break apart, about 20 minutes. Turn off the heat. (At this point, you can store the meat in the fat overnight if desired. Reheat over low heat to remelt the fat and warm the carnitas.)

Use a slotted spoon to transfer the meat to a large platter or 6 individual plates. Serve with the salsa cruda, cabbage salad, pickled jalapeños, and warm tortillas on the side.

Wrapping food in banana leaves is popular in the south of Mexico, where bananas grow like crazy. Besides protecting the food and holding it in the sauce as it cooks, the leaves impart a grassy, earthy flavor that transforms whatever is inside.

Trout is not really a traditional ingredient in Mexico (and you can actually use any white fish here), but it's a good-quality option that you can usually find all year round. The adobo can be prepared a few days in advance. The orange salad is our own little touch from Nopalito—especially delicious in the winter, when citrus is abundant.

TRUCHA ADOBADA EN HOJA DE PLÁTANO

Adobo-Rubbed Trout in Banana Leaves   ○   Serves 6 as a light meal

Adobo

6 dried guajillo chiles, stemmed and seeded

1 habanero chile

6 cloves garlic, peeled

¼ cup distilled white vinegar

3 tablespoons achiote paste (see page 26)

¼ cup rice bran oil or canola oil

Trout

1 tablespoon kosher salt

1 tablespoon sugar

Six 6-ounce pieces of trout, skin removed

Six 6-inch squares of banana leaf (from 1 to 2 large banana leaves)

Citrus Salad

3 large ripe oranges

1 tablespoon rice bran oil or canola oil

2 teaspoons freshly squeezed lime juice (from 1 lime)

Salt

¼ medium red onion, thinly sliced

Leaves from ½ bunch cilantro

6 to 12 warm soft corn tortillas, for serving (optional)

To prepare the adobo, in a medium heatproof bowl, cover the guajillo chiles with boiling water; let sit until soft, about 20 minutes.

On a griddle or small sauté pan over high heat, cook the habanero, turning frequently, until dark brown, about 15 minutes.

Transfer the habanero, garlic, vinegar, achiote paste, and the guajillo chiles (reserve the soaking water) to a blender; puree until smooth, adding a little of the soaking water only if needed to help blend. Continue to blend, streaming in the oil a little at a time, until very smooth. (The adobo will keep for a few days, refrigerated.)

To prepare the trout, add the salt and sugar to 2 cups room-temperature water and whisk well to dissolve. Add the fish to the brine and let sit for 10 minutes; remove and thoroughly pat dry. Rub the fish all over with a generous amount of the prepared adobo.

Preheat a griddle or large skillet over high heat. Add the banana leaf pieces in batches and heat until aromatic, about 5 seconds per side. Wrap one piece of fish in each leaf and fold the leaf to cover the fish. Refrigerate for at least 30 minutes or up to overnight.

When ready to serve, prepare the citrus salad: Trim off the top and bottom of each orange with a sharp knife. Stand the orange on one of its cut sides, then cut away the skin in pieces starting at the top of the orange and following the contour of the flesh with your knife. Pick up the orange and carefully cut it into wedges by slicing between the flesh and the membrane on either side. Discard the membranes.

In a large bowl, whisk together the oil, lime juice, and a pinch of salt. Add the orange wedges, onion, and cilantro leaves and toss gently to coat. Taste and adjust the seasoning if necessary.

On a large griddle or skillet over medium heat, add the banana leaf packets (no oil is needed), working in batches if necessary; cook, turning once, until the fish is just cooked through, about 10 minutes total.

Place one banana leaf on each plate and open the leaf to expose the fish. Place some of the citrus salad atop the leaf next to the fish. Serve immediately, with warm tortillas if desired.

This is a street-food sandwich, but we included it as a large plate or main course because it is a *big* antojito. There is no messing around when eating this sandwich: the bread is dunked in red salsa before being griddled, so it is saucy yet crisp, and the sandwich is warm and steaming on the inside. It's filled with hearty chorizo and potatoes, and topped with all kinds of creamy and crunchy garnishes like cabbage salad and a pickled salsa. You should be ready to get your hands messy.

TORTAS PAMBAZOS

Salsa-Dipped, Griddled Chorizo and Potato Sandwiches　○　Serves 6

¼ green cabbage, thinly shaved (about 1½ cups)

¼ white onion, thinly sliced

½ cup Crema (page 35) or sour cream

1 tablespoon kosher salt

½ cup finely diced Yukon gold potatoes (about ¾-inch pieces)

1½ cups (1 pound) crumbled Chorizo Oaxaqueño (page 44) or store-bought Mexican chorizo, casings removed

6 Teleras (Mexican Sandwich Rolls; page 36) or French rolls

Salsa Guajillo (page 233), for assembling

Rice bran oil or canola oil

¾ cup Salsa Escabeche (page 228), for spreading

1½ avocados

½ cup (12 ounces) homemade crumbled Queso Fresco (page 32) or store-bought

To make the cabbage slaw, in a bowl, combine the cabbage, onions, and crema and toss to coat. Refrigerate until ready to use.

Bring a small pot of water to a boil; add the salt and the potatoes, and let cook until al dente, 6 to 8 minutes. Drain and set aside.

In a medium skillet, cook the crumbled chorizo until hot and cooked through, about 6 minutes. Stir in the potatoes and cook for another 1 to 2 minutes to heat through.

Meanwhile, prepare the rolls so everything is hot at the same time: Slice each roll in half, not quite all the way through. Dip the outside of each roll in the salsa guajillo, making sure to coat the surface completely. In a large skillet over medium heat, drizzle in about a tablespoon of oil and add as many rolls as will fit, working in batches as needed. Cook, turning once and smashing the roll down against the surface of the pan as you cook, until the roll is seared and crispy on both outer sides (watch closely to avoid burning), about 5 minutes total. The rolls should be steaming hot when you open them, so be careful. Repeat with the remaining rolls, adding more oil as needed.

To assemble, spread 2 tablespoons of the salsa escabeche on the bottom half of each roll, then add about ¼ cup of the potato-chorizo mixture and distribute it to cover the roll evenly. Thinly slice the avocado and distribute among the sandwiches. Top with some of the cabbage slaw and sprinkle with queso fresco. Serve hot, with lots of napkins.

Chilorio, the star of this sandwich, is a northern Mexican braise of shredded pork, lard, and some sort of adobo. Most often it is made with mild chiles, but what makes this version spicy is the salsa we add, which is basically a straightforward blend of jalapeño and tomatillos. The coolness and freshness of the salsa and a crunchy cabbage salad pair perfectly with the rich elements of the chilorio and refried beans.

This sandwich is always eaten hot to prevent the pork fat from emulsifying. But you can make the meat a day or two in advance, then reheat it on a sauté pan or griddle before assembling the sandwiches.

TORTAS DE CHILORIO

Adobo-Braised Pork Sandwiches ○ Serves 6

Pork

1¼ pounds boneless pork shoulder (pork butt), cut into 4 equal pieces

Kosher salt

½ white onion, divided

2 cloves garlic

2 bay leaves

¼ medium green cabbage, shaved into thin strips

½ cup Crema (page 35) or sour cream

6 Teleras (Mexican Sandwich Rolls; page 36) or French rolls

1½ cups (12 ounces) shredded Jack cheese

1½ avocados

1½ cups (12 ounces) Frijoles Pinquitos Refritos (page 126) or store-bought refried pinto beans, warmed

Adobo for Chilorio

3 dried ancho chiles, stemmed and seeded

1 dried pasilla chile, stemmed and seeded

2 dried mulato chiles, stemmed and seeded

¾ cup white vinegar

Leaves from ½ bunch flat-leaf parsley

5 cloves garlic

1 tablespoon dried oregano

1½ teaspoons ground cumin

Kosher salt

¼ cup lard, rice bran oil, or canola oil

Salsa Jalapeño

1 to 2 jalapeños, stemmed and coarsely chopped

2 large or 4 medium tomatillos, husked and rinsed

1 teaspoon kosher salt

Season the pork all over with salt. Place the pork in a small pot and add enough water just to cover; season the water with salt and add half of the onion, the garlic, and the bay leaves. Bring to a boil, then reduce to a simmer and let cook until the meat is very tender, about 1 hour. Drain the meat and discard the liquid. Shred the meat into thin pieces (you will have about 3 cups). The pork can be made in advance and refrigerated up to 2 days.

Meanwhile, make the adobo. In a small heatproof bowl, cover all of the dried chiles with boiling water; let sit until softened, about 20 minutes. Remove the chiles (reserve the soaking water) and add to a blender with the vinegar, parsley, garlic, oregano, cumin, and a generous pinch of salt; blend until a very smooth paste forms, adding a little of the soaking water only if needed to help blend.

In a small pot, heat the lard until hot, then stir in the adobo (be careful, as it may splatter). Turn the heat down to very low and let cook, stirring occasionally, until darkened and aromatic, about 10 minutes. Stir in the shredded pork and cook for 5 minutes more to heat through. Taste and adjust the salt as needed (you can also add a little water or some of the soaking water if needed to slightly thin the consistency).

In a small blender or molcajete, quickly make the salsa jalapeño: Add the jalapeños, tomatillos, and salt and blend or grind until relatively smooth.

Thinly slice the remaining piece of white onion. In a medium bowl, mix the sliced onions and shaved cabbage with the crema and a pinch of salt, and toss to coat.

When ready to serve, preheat the oven to 350°F. Cut the rolls in half and place cut side up on a baking sheet. Sprinkle the top half of each roll with ¼ cup (2 ounces) of the Jack cheese, then bake the rolls until the cheese is melted and the bottoms are toasted, 6 to 8 minutes.

Cut the avocados into quarters, then thinly slice. Spread ¼ cup of the refried beans on the bottom half of each roll. Divide the pork among the rolls (about ½ cup each), then drizzle each with some of the salsa jalapeño to taste. Top with the sliced avocado and the cabbage slaw and serve.

Most people have heard of a *torta*—one of the traditional sandwiches of Mexico—but the *cemita* is its own unique breed of Mexican sandwich, wildly popular in Puebla, and named after the city's or the region's signature round, soft sesame buns by the same name (see page 38). In Mexico you will see cooks piling them high with breaded chicken, *lengua* (tongue), or spit-roasted pork. Often cemitas feature chipotle, Oaxacan cheese, and *pápalo*, a minty green that tastes something like a cross between arugula and cilantro. (I made it optional in this recipe because it can be hard to find fresh.)

Be sure to start the smoky, spicy Salsa de Morita several hours in advance or the day before. It requires 2 hours to simmer.

Chicken

3 boneless, skinless chicken breasts

1 cup all-purpose flour

1 tablespoon Nopalito Spices (page 35) or a mix of equal parts ground chili powder (preferably Mexican) and hot smoked paprika

1 tablespoon kosher salt

1½ teaspoons freshly ground black pepper

2 eggs

1 cup breadcrumbs

Rice bran oil or canola oil, for frying

To assemble

6 Cemitas (page 38) or another soft sandwich roll such as brioche or sesame

1½ firm-ripe avocados

¾ cup Salsa de Morita (page 222)

¼ white onion, thinly sliced

1 head romaine, trimmed and thinly sliced, or 1 bunch fresh pápalo

3 cups shredded Oaxacan cheese or mozzarella

1½ cups Mayonnaise (page 43) or store-bought mayo

1½ cups (12 ounces) Frijoles Pinquitos Refritos (page 126) or store-bought refried pinto beans

CEMITA POBLANA DE MILANESA

Breaded Chicken Sandwiches with Sesame Rolls ◦ Serves 6

Using a sharp knife, carefully slice the chicken breasts in half lengthwise. Then, one at a time, sandwich the chicken pieces between two pieces of plastic wrap, and pound with a meat pounder to ¼-inch thickness.

In a shallow mixing bowl, combine the flour, Nopalito spices, salt, and pepper. In a separate bowl, beat the eggs. Place the breadcrumbs in a third bowl. Season the chicken pieces lightly with salt. Dip each piece first into the flour mixture, turning to coat. Let any excess flour fall away, then transfer the chicken to the beaten eggs. Let any excess egg drip off, then transfer the chicken to the breadcrumbs and press to coat both sides evenly. Transfer to a platter.

Set a large paper towel–lined plate next to the stove. Heat a large skillet or griddle over medium-high heat and add 2 to 3 tablespoons oil. When the oil is hot, add 1 or 2 pieces of chicken at a time and cook, turning once, until crispy and browned on both sides and just cooked through, about 8 minutes total. Transfer to the prepared plate and repeat with the remaining chicken breasts, adding more oil as needed for each batch.

To assemble the sandwiches, preheat the oven to 350°F. Cut the rolls in half and place them cut side up on a baking sheet; bake until lightly toasted, about 5 minutes. Cut the avocados into quarters and thinly slice. Spread some of the salsa morita onto the bottom of each roll, then top with a piece of chicken, a few slices of onion, the sliced avocado, romaine, and cheese. Spread the mayonnaise and refried beans on the top half of the rolls and place on top of the sandwiches.

Fun fact: Where you are from in Mexico determines how you roll your enchiladas. In the south, we twist them into little tube shapes, but in many parts of the north they simply fold the tortilla in half (as you would a quesadilla or taco). Admittedly, it's easier to do the simple fold-over method if you're making a lot of enchiladas at once. In the south, they're almost always dipped in mole; in the north it's a variety of red and green salsas. But this one is served naked, since the "salsa flavors" are incorporated right into the chile-spiked tortillas. Without any excess sauce, you can really taste the delicate flavor of the shrimp.

If you still want a little pop of heat, drizzle the finished enchiladas with liquid from a jar of pickled jalapeños. The chile masa ingredients are needed only if you're making tortillas from scratch; otherwise, use 12 store-bought corn tortillas.

ENCHILADAS ROJAS DE CAMARÓN

Red Shrimp Enchiladas   ○   Serves 4 to 6

(If using store-bought tortillas, skip this step.) Place the guajillo chiles in a heatproof bowl and cover with boiling water; let sit until softened, about 30 minutes. Remove the chiles (reserve the soaking water) and transfer to a small blender or spice grinder; puree into a smooth, thick paste, adding only very little of the reserved soaking water if needed to help blend. In a medium bowl, mix the paste with the prepared masa and the salt. It should feel like thick, soft mashed potatoes. If it's too dense and not very malleable, add a little water.

In a large skillet, heat the oil over medium-high heat; add the onions, garlic, and jalapeño, and season with salt. Cook, stirring occasionally, until softened, about 5 minutes. Stir in the tomatoes, season lightly with salt, and bring to a boil; reduce to a simmer and let cook until some of the liquid has evaporated, 10 to 12 minutes. Season the shrimp lightly with salt and add them to the pot. Using a wooden spoon, smash the shrimp into the sauce, breaking it up into smaller pieces. Let cook just until pink, 3 to 5 minutes, then turn off the heat and let cool slightly.

(If using store-bought tortillas, skip this step.) Divide the masa into 12 portions and form each into a tortilla (see page 16).

Place the salsa guajillo in a wide bowl or on a flat plate. Sprinkle a griddle or large skillet with 2 to 3 teaspoons oil and heat over high heat. Working in batches, dip the tortillas into the salsa, coating both sides, then fry on one side for 10 seconds. Flip, then fill one side of each tortilla with ¼ cup (2 ounces) of the shrimp mixture; fold the remaining side over like a taco, and fry until no longer soggy, 1 to 2 minutes. Flip the enchilada once more and cook for an additional 1 to 2 minutes. Repeat with the remaining tortillas and filling.

To serve, place 2 or 3 enchiladas onto each of four to six plates and garnish with the crema, queso fresco, lettuce, red onion, and cilantro.

Chile Masa

4 dried guajillo chiles

2 cups Homemade Masa (page 12) or masa prepared from store-bought masa harina

½ teaspoon kosher salt, plus more as needed

Filling (Machaca de Camarón)

¼ cup rice bran oil or canola oil

1 white onion, finely chopped

2 cloves garlic, chopped

1 jalapeño, diced

2 cups canned diced tomatoes and their juices

1 pound fresh shrimp, peeled, deveined, and coarsely chopped

To assemble

Salsa Guajillo (page 233)

Rice bran oil or canola oil, for pan-frying

For serving

Crema (page 35) or sour cream

Crumbled queso fresco

Shaved iceberg lettuce

¼ red onion, thinly sliced

Chopped fresh cilantro leaves

This mole is the characteristic sauce from Puebla, Mexico. It is a go-to dish for special occasions in the region, where it is a spectacle to watch being made: sometimes as many as twenty old women will be working on the same mole at any one time, turning out gallons over a wood fire.

There are a lot of ingredients, but surprisingly, you can taste each one in the sauce: the fruity and spicy nuances of the chiles, the smoky char from the toasted bread, and the sweetness from the Mexican chocolate. Start the process in the morning or the day before. In Mexico we say *el recalentado es mejor*—"it tastes even better when reheated."

ENCHILADAS DE MOLE POBLANO

Chicken Enchiladas with Mole Poblano ○ Serves 6

Place the chicken in a large pot and add enough water just to cover. Add the onion, garlic, bay leaves, and 1 tablespoon of the salt. Bring to a boil, then reduce to a simmer; let cook, occasionally skimming away any fat or foam from the top of the broth, until the meat is fully cooked through, about 45 minutes.

Remove the chicken (reserve the cooking liquid) and let rest until cool enough to handle. Pull and shred the meat from the bones. Strain the liquid through a fine-mesh strainer and reserve. (These steps can be done up to 2 days ahead.)

Preheat the oven to 350°F. Meanwhile, heat a large skillet over high heat and add all of the dried whole chiles; cook, turning often with tongs, until they darken and blister but do not burn, 1 to 2 minutes total. Transfer the chiles to a heatproof bowl and cover with boiling water. Let soak until softened, about 20 minutes.

On a small baking sheet, combine the sesame seeds, almonds, peanuts, pepitas, raisins, prunes, coriander seeds, anise seeds, sliced bread, and piece of tortilla if using; roast, stirring occasionally and watching for burning, until the seeds and nuts are toasted, about 15 minutes. Remove and let cool.

In the large skillet, heat 2 tablespoons of the oil over medium heat and add the plantain. Fry, turning the slices occasionally, until golden brown all over, about 10 minutes.

In a medium pot, heat 2 tablespoons of the oil over medium heat and add the onions and garlic, season with salt. Cook, stirring occasionally, until the onions are translucent, about 5 minutes. Add the tomatoes and tomatillos, season with salt and bring to a boil, then reduce to a simmer. Cover and let cook for 15 minutes. Turn off the heat and set aside.

Chicken

1 whole (3- to 4-pound) chicken

½ white onion

4 cloves garlic

2 bay leaves

1 tablespoon kosher salt

Mole

½ cup sesame seeds

½ cup almonds

¾ cup peanuts

¾ cup pepitas

¾ cup raisins

½ cup pitted prunes

¾ teaspoon coriander seeds

¼ teaspoon anise seeds

¼ small French roll, thinly sliced, or the equivalent of any soft white bread (about ¼ cup bread)

¼ soft corn tortilla (optional)

4 dried mulato chiles, stemmed and seeded

2 dried pasilla chiles, stemmed and seeded

CONTINUED

CONTINUED

2 dried chiles negros, stemmed and seeded

1 dried ancho chile, stemmed and seeded

¼ cup plus 3 tablespoons rice bran oil or canola oil, divided

½ plantain, sliced into ½-inch-thick rounds

1 white onion, chopped

4 cloves garlic

1½ cups (12 ounces) canned diced tomatoes and their juices

5 tomatillos, husked and coarsely chopped

1 Chipotle Adobado (page 42) or 1 canned store-bought chipotle in adobo

½ cinnamon stick

1 tablespoon sugar

1½ (3.1-ounce) disks Mexican chocolate (preferably Ibarra or Abuelita brand), chopped

Salt, as needed

18 homemade soft corn tortillas (see page 16) or store-bought tortillas

For serving

Toasted sesame seeds

Crumbled queso fresco

Sliced white onion

Remove the chiles (discard the soaking water) and place in a blender. Add the contents of the baking sheet and puree, using a little of the chicken cooking liquid only as needed, until very smooth. Add the fried plantain, the onion-tomato mixture, and the chipotle in adobo, and blend until very smooth. Set aside.

In a large pot, heat the remaining 3 tablespoons oil over high heat. Turn off the heat and quickly pour in the contents of the blender all at once. Let fry, stirring constantly, 10 minutes. Add the cinnamon and about 2 cups more of the reserved chicken cooking liquid and bring to a simmer; cook for 15 minutes, then stir in the sugar and chocolate. Cook until the chocolate is melted, then taste the mole and adjust the seasoning as needed. Let simmer for 30 minutes or until some of the oil starts rising to the top. (That is the indication that the mole is done.)

When ready to serve, mix the chicken meat with the warm mole and cook gently until the meat is warmed through.

To assemble, preheat a clean large skillet or griddle over medium heat; add the tortillas in batches in a single layer and cook, turning once, until heated through and softened, about 4 minutes. Stack the tortillas on a platter, board, or clean work surface and cover with a towel to keep warm. Spoon about ¼ cup (2 ounces) of the chicken-mole mixture in a line down the center of each, and fold the tortillas in half or roll them into tube shapes to enclose the filling. Serve 3 enchiladas per plate, and spoon more mole on top to cover. Garnish with sesame seeds, queso fresco, and white onion.

Feel free to use any combination of seasonal vegetables when making these colorful, healthful enchiladas. We chose a mix that would offer lots of contrast in color and texture, but you can also focus on even one vegetable you love or happen to have a lot of in the fridge. For example, we've featured them on our menu filled with loads of delicious sautéed Swiss chard.

These enchiladas go perfectly with a side of Mexican rice. And the accompanying medium-heat green salsa recipe makes a little extra, because once you have some on hand, you'll use it on everything: with chips as an appetizer, alongside fried or poached eggs, and atop tacos and braised meats.

ENCHILADAS VEGETARIANAS

Vegetable Enchiladas with Cilantro Salsa   ○   Serves 6

1 cup rice bran oil or canola oil, divided

1 cup finely diced white onion

½ teaspoon chopped fresh garlic

Salt

1½ cups diced peeled carrots

1½ cups small cauliflower florets

1½ cups finely diced zucchini

1½ cups thinly sliced trimmed asparagus

5 cups (2½ batches) Salsa Cilantro (page 218)

12 homemade soft corn tortillas (see page 16) or store-bought tortillas

3 cups shredded Jack cheese

Arroz Mexicano (page 122; optional)

Preheat the oven to 400°F. In a large ovenproof skillet or Dutch oven, heat ¼ cup of the oil over medium heat. Add the onions and garlic and season with salt. Cook, stirring occasionally, until translucent, about 5 minutes. Add the carrots, cauliflower, zucchini, and asparagus, and raise the heat to high; cook, stirring occasionally, for 2 minutes. Transfer the pan to the oven and roast until the vegetables are al dente, about 5 minutes. Transfer back to the stove and pour the cilantro salsa over the top; bring to a boil, then turn off the heat. Taste and adjust the seasoning as necessary.

Lower the oven temperature to 350°F. Set a paper towel–lined baking sheet next to the stove. In a large skillet, heat the remaining ¾ cup oil. Add the tortillas, 1 or 2 at a time, and fry just until soft, 30 seconds per side. Remove and transfer to the prepared baking sheet to absorb some of the oil.

Working on a platter, board, or clean work surface, spoon about ¼ cup (2 ounces) of the vegetable and salsa mixture down the center of each tortilla, then fold in half or roll into a tube shape to enclose the filling. Transfer to a large casserole dish, overlapping the tortillas slightly if you went with the folding method. Pour any remaining filling and salsa on top of the enchiladas, making sure to distribute it evenly. Sprinkle the Jack cheese evenly on top and transfer the dish to the oven; bake until the cheese is fully melted, about 10 minutes.

Using a spatula, transfer 2 of the enchiladas onto each of 6 plates. Serve with a side of rice if desired.

10 dried guajillo chiles,
stemmed and seeded

5 dried ancho chiles,
stemmed and seeded

4 dried morita chiles,
stemmed

½ cup sesame seeds, plus
more for garnish

¼ cup almonds

½ small French roll, thinly
sliced, or the equivalent of
any soft white bread (about
½ cup bread)

½ soft corn tortilla
(optional)

¼ teaspoon ground
cinnamon

½ teaspoon dried oregano

1½ teaspoons dried
marjoram

¼ teaspoon ground allspice

½ teaspoon freshly ground
black pepper

1 cup rice bran oil or
canola oil

3 cloves garlic

½ white onion, diced

½ teaspoon kosher salt,
plus more as needed

½ plantain, sliced into
½-inch-thick rounds

5 medium tomatillos, husked
and coarsely chopped

2 cups (16 ounces) canned
diced tomatoes and their
juices

¾ cup sugar

1½ (3.1-ounce) disks Mexican
chocolate (preferably Ibarra
or Abuelita brand), chopped

Homemade soft corn
tortillas (see page 16) or
store-bought soft corn
tortillas

Toasted sesame seeds

Sliced white onion

The name *coloradito* refers to Colorado and its red rocks—which are close to the color of this mole. Serving tortillas dipped in it is a classic preparation in Mexico, but you can of course add shredded pork or chicken, sliced duck, cooked shrimp, or white fish to the dish.

The secret to mole's matchless flavor is in spending the time to blend so many little ingredients into the mole, cook it low and slow, then quick-fry it in smoking-hot oil. Taking shortcuts is kind of like running down the street with one shoe: you can certainly do it, but it won't be the very best experience you can have.

ENMOLADAS DE COLORADITO

Tortillas in Mole Coloradito with Sesame and Onion ○ Serves 8 to 10

Preheat the oven to 350°F. Meanwhile, heat a griddle or large skillet over high heat. Add the guajillo, ancho, and morita chiles, working in batches if needed, and cook, turning every 10 seconds, until blistered but not burnt, 30 to 40 seconds. Transfer to a heatproof bowl and cover with boiling water; let soak until softened, about 20 minutes.

On a small baking sheet, distribute the sesame seeds, almonds, bread, tortilla (if using), cinnamon, oregano, marjoram, allspice, pepper; roast, stirring occasionally and checking for burning, until the ingredients are toasted, about 20 minutes.

In a medium pot, heat ¼ cup of the oil over medium heat. Add the garlic, onions, and salt and cook, stirring occasionally, until the onions are softened, about 10 minutes (lower the heat if the onions begin to brown). Add the tomatillos and tomatoes and bring to a low simmer; cook, stirring occasionally, for 30 minutes more. Turn off the heat and set aside.

Meanwhile, in a medium skillet, heat another ¼ cup of the oil over medium heat and add the plantain. Fry, turning the pieces occasionally, until golden brown, 6 to 8 minutes.

Transfer the contents of the baking sheet to a blender. Add the reconstituted chiles (reserve the soaking water) and puree, adding a little of the soaking water if needed to blend. Add the onion-tomato mixture and the plantain and season with salt. Blend, working in batches if needed, until very smooth. (At this point, the mole can be cooled and refrigerated overnight or up to 3 days.)

To fry the mole, an hour before serving, heat the remaining ½ cup of the oil in a large pot or Dutch oven until smoking hot. Turn off the heat and pour in the sauce quickly and all at once (be careful, as the oil may splatter), then turn the heat back on and bring the mole to a boil. Reduce to a simmer and let cook for 30 minutes. Stir in the sugar, chocolate, and a little water only if needed for consistency (it should not be too thick) and cook for 30 minutes more. Taste and add more salt if needed.

When ready to serve, dip the warm tortillas in the hot mole using tongs; transfer them to serving plates and fold them in half. Top with sesame seeds and sliced onions, and serve.

Braising is the most popular way to serve large cuts of meat in Mexico, and it works well for *costillas*, or pork ribs: After a few hours of simmering in the oven, the ribs come out so tender the meat practically falls off the bone. Traditionally, costillas de puerco are mixed into a green salsa, which, when combined with cooked cactus (*nopales*), contributes a surprising amount of the bulk of this dish. You really need only one rib per person (but then again, we don't blame you if you want a second once you have a taste).

You can serve costillas with a side of Frijoles Negros de la Olla (page 126) and Arroz Mexicano (page 122) for a more filling meal.

It's worth the effort to seek out the avocado leaves, which are used to flavor the braise, at Mexican markets or online—their unique anise-y flavor adds that special something to the dish. But in a pinch, you can skip them. If you can't find fresh cactus, you can try substituting purslane.

1½ large white onions, peeled

10 medium tomatillos, husked and rinsed

4 jalapeños, stemmed

4 cloves garlic, peeled

2 tablespoons rice bran oil or canola oil

2 pounds pork spare ribs, sliced into individual ribs

Kosher salt

3 medium nopales (about 1⅓ pounds), spines trimmed, diced into ½-inch squares or 6 cups purslane

2 fresh or dried avocado leaves (optional)

Leaves from ¼ bunch cilantro

12 to 18 soft corn tortillas, warmed (optional)

Black beans and/or rice (optional)

COSTILLAS DE PUERCO EN SALSA VERDE CON NOPALES

Stewed Pork Ribs and Cactus with Salsa Verde   ○   Serves 6

Preheat the oven to 350°F. Slice the whole onion and place it on a baking sheet. Add the tomatillos, jalapeños, and 2 cloves of the garlic and roast, stirring occasionally, until the tomatillos are wrinkled and the onions are browned in spots, 30 minutes.

Meanwhile, in a large pot or Dutch oven, heat 2 tablespoons of the oil over medium-high heat until hot but not smoking. Season the ribs generously all over with salt and, working in batches as needed to avoid crowding, add the ribs in a single layer to the pot; cook, turning occasionally, until the meat is seared on all sides, about 8 minutes. Pour off the fat and reserve 3 tablespoons for frying the salsa later.

Lower the heat to 325°F. Add enough water to the pot to just cover the pork ribs. Add the remaining ½ onion and 2 cloves garlic, and the avocado leaves if using. Cover the pot and transfer to the oven; let cook until the meat is very tender, about 2½ hours.

While the meat cooks, make the salsa: In a food processor or molcajete, combine the roasted tomatillos, jalapeños, and garlic, and a generous pinch of salt; pulse or grind until chunky. Set the salsa aside until the pork is done.

Fill a 9-inch skillet two-thirds full with water and bring to a boil. Add a generous pinch of salt and the nopales; cook until tender, about 5 minutes, then drain and set aside.

When the ribs are done braising, drain (discard the liquid) and reserve the ribs on a platter; let the pot cool slightly, then carefully dry out the inside. Add the reserved pork fat and heat over medium-high heat. Pour in the salsa quickly and all at once (be careful, as the oil may splatter) and cook until simmering, about 2 minutes. Add the pork and the cactus and cook, stirring to coat everything in the salsa, until the meat is heated through. Stir in the cilantro. Taste and add more salt if needed.

Serve the pork ribs with warm tortillas and black beans or rice if desired.

This is a classic Mexican side dish that couldn't be simpler to make. The crisp cabbage and sharp lime dressing make it perfect for pairing with richer dishes like carnitas or fried fish, but you wouldn't really eat it as a salad on its own. Unlike many lettuce-based salads, leftovers of this salad will keep for a day in the fridge.

1 cup freshly squeezed lime juice (from 6 to 8 limes)

1 tablespoon dried oregano

1½ teaspoons kosher salt

8 cups sliced green cabbage (½-inch ribbons)

2 peeled carrots, shaved into ribbons with a vegetable peeler

ENSALADA DE REPOLLO

Sliced Cabbage Salad ○ Serves 8

Whisk the lime juice, oregano, and salt until the salt is completely dissolved. In a large bowl, combine the cabbage and carrots. Add the liquid mixture and taste for salt. Let it sit for 15 minutes, taste again for salt, and serve.

Bebidas y Postres

(DRINKS & DESSERTS)

SWEETS HAVE A SPECIAL PLACE IN MEXICAN CULTURE

although, unlike elsewhere in the world, they are not always eaten as dessert. When I was a boy, the late afternoon, that long stretch between lunch and dinner when the sun was at its hottest, was when many Mexican farmers and laborers would need energy and reach for something sweet. Most often this meant a cold *agua fresca* made by blending locally grown fruits or basic pantry staples such as rice or nuts into a drink with sugar and water, or *paletas* (popsicles) from a similar mashup of ingredients. Where I grew up, some fancier restaurants offered flan on their menus, and street vendors sometimes sold churros, but beyond that, the most effort we would spend on dessert was occasionally candying some sweet potatoes in caramel or whisking up a mug of frothy Mexican hot chocolate. The recipes in this section contain a little something from each of those sweet spectrums, all easy and relatively quick to make for home cooks.

At the time I left Mexico, there was not much of a cocktail culture where I was raised. For locals, drinking mostly meant sipping on straight tequila or cracking open a cold Mexican beer. I'm sure that is changing in some parts of Mexico, and at Nopalito, cocktails and desserts have been a fun and playful part of our San Francisco restaurant culture, and well represented on the menu from the start. Most are made with easy-to-find ingredients you can access year-round. I love that they give a creative charge to some of the classic flavors of old-world Mexico.

Aguas frescas come in a wide range of flavors in Mexico, since we traditionally used whatever we had available: sometimes orange juice with a little sugar and water, sometimes tropical fruits like bananas blended and diluted, and oftentimes dried rice steeped overnight in water to soften and blend into a milky version we call *horchata*. We always have a variety of them on the menu at Nopalito.

In our restaurant version we use organic brown rice, incorporate almonds for a nuttier flavor, and use agave nectar instead of sugar (it blends more easily). The nuts make for a richer consistency than you'd find in a typical agua fresca, somewhere between a glass of milk and a smoothie.

HORCHATA

1¼ cups cooked long-grain brown rice, preferably organic

1 cup raw almonds

¾ cup plus 2 tablespoons agave nectar

¼ teaspoon freshly ground cinnamon

Oaxacan-Style Horchata

1 cup cleaned and stemmed strawberries

½ cup agave nectar

1½ teaspoons freshly squeezed lime juice

¼ teaspoon kosher salt

Horchata (preceding recipe)

Serves 6

Pour 3 cups water into the bowl of a blender or a large mixing bowl and add the brown rice, almonds, agave nectar, and cinnamon. Let soak overnight. Blend in a high-powered blender until smooth, then mix with an additional 6 cups water. Strain through a fine-mesh strainer. Serve over ice.

Oaxacan-Style Horchata

In a blender, combine the strawberries, agave nectar, lime juice, and salt; blend this syrup until smooth.

For each serving, fill up a 12-ounce glass with ice and fill three-quarters of the way with horchata. Pour 2 ounces Oaxacan-style syrup on top.

We prepare this drink in big batches in Mexico, since its saturated magenta color and fruity, floral quality make it a real crowd-pleaser, and you can drink it over the course of a day or two. You can find dried hibiscus flowers at many Mexican markets, in the bulk bins at some health food stores, or online.

AGUA DE JAMAICA

Hibiscus and Valencia Orange Agua Fresca　◦　Serves 4 to 6

½ cup agave nectar

2½ cups (2½ ounces) dried hibiscus flowers

1 cup freshly squeezed orange juice (from 3 to 4 oranges)

1½ teaspoons freshly squeezed lime juice

In a small pot, bring 2 cups water to a boil. Add the agave nectar and hibiscus flowers. Turn off the heat and let steep for 30 minutes; strain and let cool completely. Add the orange juice, lime juice, and an additional 4 cups water.

Taste and adjust the sweetness and acidity as necessary. Serve over ice.

We decided not to serve sodas at Nopalito, but we liked the idea of having as an option a lemon-lime-style drink that's less cloying than a traditional bottled soda. We went with an all-lime version sweetened lightly with agave syrup that's balanced with the spicy kick of freshly pureed ginger.

Serve within 2 days for best quality.

LIMONADA DE LIMÓN Y GENGIBRE

Ginger Limeade　◦　Serves 6

½ cup peeled, diced fresh ginger

½ cup agave nectar

½ teaspoon kosher salt

1 cup freshly squeezed lime juice (from 6 to 8 limes), plus zest of 1 lime

In a blender, combine the ginger, 1 cup water, the agave nectar, and the salt; blend until smooth, then strain through a fine-mesh strainer. Add the lime juice, lime zest, and an additional 8 cups water. Serve over ice (if not serving with ice, you may need to add more water).

During the few weeks when strawberries hit their peak of sweetness and saturated color, I can't resist them in agua fresca. This version lets the straightforward flavor of the fruit shine, with just a touch of salt, lime juice, and agave nectar to enhance it.

LIMONADA DE LIMÓN Y FRESA

Strawberry Limeade   ○   Serves 10

4 cups stemmed, chopped strawberries, plus 1 cup sliced, for serving (optional)

1¾ cups agave nectar

1 teaspoon kosher salt

2 cups freshly squeezed lime juice (from about 12 limes)

In a blender, combine the chopped strawberries, 2 cups water, the agave nectar, and the salt; puree until smooth. Transfer to a pitcher and add 6 cups water and the lime juice. Top with the sliced strawberries if using.

Coffee in Mexico was traditionally brewed in a large *olla*, or clay pot. Unlike in the States, where we're used to customizing our own cup with sweetener or milk, café de la olla is classically made in one big batch presweetened with piloncillo and seasoned with spices like cinnamon, anise, and cloves. To simplify the process, I altered the brewing to be a hands-off cold-brew preparation instead of hot. Since the coffee is dark and spicy, a little milk and ice take the edge off.

ICED CAFÉ DE LA OLLA

Mexican Spiced Iced Coffee   ○   Serves 6

To make the syrup, combine the piloncillo and 1 cup water in a small pot. Bring to a boil, then remove from the heat and let cool completely; the piloncillo should be completely melted by the time the water is fully cooled.

To a large coffee filter or double layer of cheesecloth, add the coffee, anise, cloves, cinnamon, and orange; wrap the ingredients fully with the filter or cheesecloth and secure to form a sealed bundle. Submerge in 7 cups water and let steep 8 hours. Remove the bundle and squeeze it out into the water to extract all the flavor. Whisk in ¾ cup of the piloncillo syrup.

For each serving, pour 8 ounces of the coffee over ice and add 2 ounces milk.

Syrup

1 medium (8-ounce) cone piloncillo or 1½ cups brown sugar

Coffee

½ pound coffee, ground

½ teaspoon anise seeds

¼ teaspoon cloves

¼ cup plus 2 tablespoons ground cinnamon

½ orange, peeled

1½ cups whole milk, for serving

A big mug of dense, spicy hot chocolate is traditional in Mexico on cooler nights or mornings—especially for my family, since my grandfather used to grow cacao and we always had a fresh supply. Traditionally, the Mexican version contains hot milk and Mexican chocolate (which is flavored with sugar and cinnamon), whisked until foamy using a molinillo (see page 49). I loved the tradition so much, I got a tattoo of a molinillo.

We fancied up the classic recipe with a pinch of salt, some hot chiles, and a little orange zest, and you don't need a molinillo to make it—any kitchen whisk will do. If serving to kids, you can leave out some or all of the chiles.

CHOCOLATE CON CHILES

Hot Chocolate with Chiles   ◦   Serves 8

5 cups whole milk

1½ cups heavy cream

1½ teaspoons vanilla extract

¼ cup sugar

¼ teaspoon kosher salt

1 cinnamon stick, preferably Mexican

Stripped zest of 1 orange

1 ancho chile, seeded

1 guajillo chile, seeded

1½ chiles de arból, seeded

16 ounces bittersweet chocolate (70% cacao), chopped

In a medium pot, combine the milk, cream, vanilla, sugar, and salt. Add the cinnamon, orange zest, and chiles, and bring the mixture to a boil. Lower the heat to a simmer and cook for 20 minutes. Strain the hot liquid through a fine-mesh sieve. Add the chocolate and stir until dissolved. Let stand 5 minutes, then whisk with a molinillo or standard whisk until foamy. Serve hot in mugs.

This is our Mexico-inspired twist on a classic cocktail called the Bee's Knees, a light and refreshing drink made with gin, lemon, and honey syrup. The Killer Bee replaces the gin with mezcal, a darker, smokier, and more aggressive spirit (hence the more aggressive cocktail name). It's a great way to kick off a meal.

KILLER BEE

Makes 1

1½ ounces honey

2 ounces mezcal, such as Del Maguey Vida brand

1½ ounces freshly squeezed lemon juice (from 1 lemon)

Ice

To make a honey syrup, in a small bowl or jar, combine the honey with 1½ ounces water.

In a cocktail shaker, combine the mezcal, lemon juice, and ¾ ounce of the honey syrup (save the remaining honey syrup for another cocktail). Fill the shaker three-quarters of the way with ice and shake vigorously for 10 seconds if serving on the rocks or 15 seconds if serving "up." Strain into an ice-filled double old-fashioned glass or bucket glass, or serve up with no ice.

This old-school tequila cocktail has been making a bit of a comeback. Flavor-wise, it is driven by its three main ingredients: tequila, naturally spicy ginger beer (we use Bundaberg brand), and fresh lime juice. But the subtle accent is the crème de cassis, a black currant liqueur that gives the drink a slight pink hue and the faintest fruity flavor.

EL DIABLO

Makes 1

2 ounces blanco tequila, such as Pueblo Viejo brand

¾ ounce freshly squeezed lime juice, plus finely grated lime zest for garnish

Ice

3 ounces ginger beer, such as Bundaberg brand

1 to 2 dashes crème de cassis or another berry cordial

Add the tequila and lime juice to a cocktail shaker. Add a small amount of ice, and shake once quickly (just to chill, not dilute).

Strain into a Collins glass and add the ginger beer and crème de cassis. Add ice and garnish with the lime zest.

1 ounce agave nectar

Kosher salt (optional)

2 ounces blanco tequila, such as Pueblo Viejo brand

1 ounce freshly squeezed lime juice (from 1 to 2 limes)

½ ounce orange liqueur, such as Combier brand

Ice

At Nopalito we make our margaritas fresh, bright, and tequila-forward, erring on the dry rather than the sweet side. A small amount of agave syrup takes the edge off all the bracingly tart fresh lime juice.

MARGARITA

Makes 1

To make an agave syrup, in a small bowl or jar, combine the agave nectar and 1 ounce water.

If desired, salt the rim of a rocks glass by dipping it in a shallow bowl of water, then twisting it in a small pile of salt.

In a cocktail shaker, combine the tequila, lime juice, orange liqueur, and ¼ ounce of the agave syrup (save the remaining agave syrup for more margaritas). Fill the shaker three-quarters of the way with ice and shake vigorously for 10 seconds if serving on the rocks or 15 seconds if serving "up." Strain into an ice-filled rocks glass or serve up with no ice.

The traditional paloma is a simple cocktail made with tequila, grapefruit soda, and a dash of salt and lime. We use fresh grapefruit and swap out the tequila for mezcal, its smokier cousin. But it's the couple of dashes of Cynar, an artichoke-based bittersweet Italian liqueur, that turns our paloma into something special. Its bitter and vegetal qualities give a more sophisticated contrast to the finished cocktail.

MEZCAL PALOMA

Makes 1

2 ounces agave nectar

1½ ounces mezcal, such as Del Maguey Vida brand

1½ ounces freshly squeezed grapefruit juice, plus one strip grapefruit peel (from 1 grapefruit)

½ ounce freshly squeezed lime juice (from 1 lime)

Ice

2 ounces soda water

1 to 2 dashes Cynar (optional but highly recommended)

To make an agave syrup, in a small bowl or jar, combine the agave nectar with 2 ounces water.

In a cocktail shaker, combine the mezcal, grapefruit juice, lime juice, and ½ ounce of the agave syrup (save the remaining agave syrup for more cocktails). Add a small amount of ice and shake once quickly (just to chill, not dilute).

Strain into a glass, then top off with soda water. Add fresh ice and top with Cynar if using. Squeeze the grapefruit peel, skin side down, over the finished cocktail to release the grapefruit oils; discard the peel.

1 cup agave nectar

1½ cups blanco tequila,
such as Pueblo Viejo brand

¾ cup freshly squeezed lemon
juice (from 2 to 3 lemons)

½ cup Campari

Ice

Vivid, lemony, and just the right amount of bitter, this cocktail is named for the blanco tequila and red-tinged Campari it contains. You can stir everything together before friends arrive, then shake or stir individual drinks with ice when ready to serve.

BLANCO ROJO

Serves 8

To make an agave syrup, in a pitcher, combine the agave nectar with 1 cup water; stir well. Add the tequila, lemon juice, and Campari.

When ready to serve, fill a cocktail shaker three-quarters full with ice and shake a scant 1 cup of the mixture at a time for 10 seconds if serving on the rocks or 15 seconds if serving "up."

Strain the shaken mixture into 2 ice-filled double old-fashioned glasses or bucket glasses, or serve up without ice. Repeat with the remaining cocktail mixture.

**Orange Zest
Whipped Cream**

½ ounce agave nectar

8 ounces heavy cream

Zest of ½ orange

Drink

1 ounce añejo tequila,
such as Siete Leguas
brand

½ ounce coffee
liqueur, such as Araku
or Kahlua brand

Hot brewed coffee
(about 4 ounces)

Ground cinnamon
(preferably freshly
ground), to garnish

This is a short but mighty cocktail that packs a good flavor punch. The base spirit is añejo tequila, an aged variety that offers more warm-spice characteristics than your average tequila, due to its time spent in barrel. We add a small amount of coffee liqueur to sweeten and balance the drink and also to boost the intensity of the coffee flavor. The coffee itself makes this a stick of dynamite after dinner.

MEXICAN COFFEE

Makes 1

To make the whipped cream, in a medium mixing bowl, combine the agave nectar with ½ ounce (1 tablespoon) water. Add the cream and zest and whisk vigorously, or beat with an electric mixer until soft peaks form.

Warm a small (6-ounce) coffee cup by filling it with hot water. Empty the cup and add the tequila and coffee liqueur, then add hot coffee to fill. Top with a dollop of the whipped cream, and garnish with a light dusting of cinnamon, or more to taste.

At its base, our house Bloody Maria "mix" is a trinity of tomato juice, orange juice, and the smoked jalapeño vinegar that we think is an indispensable part of this cocktail. The combination results in the perfect balance of texture, sweetness, acidity, and smoky spice—and frankly, without smoking the chiles, you risk a less interesting drink. If you don't have a smoker, it is worth the effort to rig one up on your stove top (see page 78) or research how to rig one up on your grill.

Smoked Jalapeño Vinegar

3 medium jalapeños, halved lengthwise

Apple cider vinegar

Sangrita

16 ounces (2 cups) tomato juice

8 ounces (1 cup) freshly squeezed orange juice (from 2 to 3 oranges)

8 ounces (1 cup) Smoked Jalapeño Vinegar (above), or to taste based on the heat of the jalapeños

Salt, to taste

12 ounces (1½ cups) blanco tequila, such as Pueblo Viejo brand

Ice

For serving

Kosher salt (optional)

Lemon wedges

BLOODY MARIA

Makes 8

To make the vinegar, preheat a smoker (see page 78) using almond wood chips or another wood chip you like. Add the jalapeños and smoke for 3 hours. Remove and let cool fully.

Transfer the jalapeños to a blender and add just enough apple cider vinegar to cover; blend until smooth, add salt to taste. Store in an airtight container up to 5 days.

To make the sangrita, in a pitcher, combine the tomato juice, orange juice, and jalapeño vinegar; stir well. (Sangrita will keep in an airtight container in the refrigerator for up to 5 days.) Add the tequila to the pitcher and stir briefly. Add a good amount of ice to chill the mixture briefly.

If desired, salt the rim of eight glasses by dipping them in a shallow bowl of water, then twisting them one by one into a small pile of salt. Fill the glasses with fresh ice and strain the cocktail mixture over the ice. Squeeze a lemon wedge on top of each, then drop a wedge into each glass, and serve.

You'll come across a variety of flans in restaurants in Mexico, including flavored styles like strawberry, chocolate, and lemon. But my favorite has always been flan Napolitano, the classic custard made with condensed and evaporated milk topped with a thin layer of caramel. I added some orange zest, since to me, dessert needs a pop of acidity from something like citrus (as well as a little salt) to tame and balance the sweet flavors.

When you check to see if your flan is ready, the surface should be totally creamy-looking, with no bubbles (a sign of overcooked flan).

FLAN NAPOLITANO

Serves 6 to 8

½ cup sugar

3 large eggs, at room temperature

½ vanilla bean, seeds scraped out

1 (14-ounce) can sweetened condensed milk

1 (12-ounce) can evaporated milk

Finely grated zest of 1 small orange

½ teaspoon kosher salt

Preheat the oven to 350°F. Boil enough water to fill the bottom of the roasting pan in which the flan will be steamed.

To make the caramel, in a small pot over medium-low heat, melt the sugar. Cook, swirling the pan occasionally, until the caramel turns deep golden amber, 8 to 10 minutes. Immediately pour into a 9-inch round cake pan and swirl to coat the bottom. Set aside and let the caramel set slightly.

In a blender or a large mixing bowl, beat the eggs with the seeds of the vanilla bean. Add the condensed milk, evaporated milk, zest, and salt and blend well. Pour the mixture on top of the caramel in the cake pan.

Set the cake pan inside a roasting pan. Pour in enough boiling water to reach halfway up the sides of the cake pan containing the flan. Cover the whole roasting pan in aluminum foil and bake until the sides of the flan are set but the middle is ever so slightly jiggly when shaken, 45 minutes to 1 hour. (A toothpick inserted into the center of the flan should come out clean.)

Remove the roasting pan, then lift out the cake pan and let cool completely on a wire rack (at this point you can refrigerate the flan until the next day). Once the flan has fully cooled, run a knife around the edges of the pan to help release it. Carefully but quickly invert the flan onto a serving plate.

Because everyone who comes to a Mexican restaurant expects there to be churros, we had to have them on the menu. This easy recipe is adapted from the one from my favorite street vendors back home and yields thin, puffy, lightly crispy churros. If you don't have a *churrera* or a piping bag, you can cut a corner off the end of a plastic freezer bag and use that to pipe your churros, but they won't have the great ridges for catching the cinnamon sugar, and you may have to adjust your cooking time to account for the difference in size.

Churros are best when served fresh, but if necessary you can hold them in a warm oven until serving time. They are great for dipping in Chocolate con Chiles (page 190).

CHURROS MEXICANOS

Makes 6 thick churros, or 12 skinny churros

½ cup (1 stick) unsalted butter

1 cup plus 1 tablespoon sugar

1 teaspoon kosher salt

2 teaspoons ground cinnamon

1 cup all-purpose flour

3 eggs, beaten

4 cups rice bran oil or canola oil, for frying

In a medium pot, combine 1 cup water, the butter, 1 tablespoon sugar, the salt, and 1 teaspoon of the cinnamon; cook over medium heat until the butter is melted, then turn off the heat. Add the flour all at once and mix, using a wooden spoon, until just incorporated. Let cool for about 15 minutes (check that it's cool enough to the touch that it won't cook the eggs), then stir in the eggs.

Transfer the dough to a churrera or to a piping bag fitted with a wide, round, or open-starred tip. In a medium bowl, combine the remaining 1 cup sugar and 1 teaspoon cinnamon.

Set a paper towel–lined plate next to the stove. In a deep fryer, large pot, or high-sided skillet, heat the oil to 375°F. Pipe 6-inch churros into the oil, frying a few at a time without overcrowding the pan. Let fry, turning occasionally to cook evenly, until deep golden brown, 3 to 7 minutes total, depending on the thickness of the churro. Remove the churros and transfer briefly to the prepared plate. Quickly transfer the hot churros from the plate to the bowl of cinnamon-sugar mixture; toss to coat the churros. Serve hot.

These simple, delicious cookies get their name from their signature crumbly consistency (*polvo* means "dust" in Spanish). The key is using cake flour, which is lighter in protein than all-purpose flour, so it naturally creates a finer crumb. We bake the flour in the oven first to give it a lightly toasted flavor.

These cookies are great for anytime but go especially well with a cup of coffee after a meal.

POLVORONES

Mexican Wedding Cookies ○ Makes about 4 dozen small cookies

½ cup raw almonds

3¾ cups (18 ounces) cake flour, such as Snowflake brand self-rising cake flour

¼ cup granulated sugar

¾ teaspoon baking powder

¾ teaspoon kosher salt

¾ teaspoon ground cinnamon

10 ounces (2½ sticks) unsalted butter, melted

¾ teaspoon vanilla extract

Powdered sugar, for dusting

Preheat the oven to 375°F. Add the almonds to a small baking sheet, and add the flour to a separate small baking sheet; bake both until the almonds are toasted and the flour is a dark cream color, about 20 minutes. Remove and let cool completely (otherwise the almonds will turn to almond butter when ground). Lower the heat to 350°F.

In a food processor, combine the cooled almonds, sugar, baking powder, salt, and cinnamon and process until the almonds are finely ground.

Transfer the mixture to a stand mixer fitted with the paddle attachment, or to a large bowl, and beat in the melted butter and vanilla on low speed. Add the toasted flour and mix on low speed until just incorporated.

Line a couple of baking sheets with parchment paper. Using a small cookie scoop or melon baller, place level scoops of dough on the prepared pans 1½ inches apart. Bake, rotating the pans halfway through, until evenly browned and cooked through, about 30 minutes. Remove and dust with powdered sugar while still hot. Let cool completely; these will keep for several days if stored in an airtight container.

Nopalito
9th Ave.
1224 9th Ave
415-233-9966

05/04/2016

Server: Angela
Cashier: Blair
Table 36/1
Guests: 3
Reprint #: 2

G1 Horse & P   (3 @11,0
G1 La Follette (2 @11,0
Totopos
Quesadilla Roja
Tacos de Pescado (2
Side Crema

Subtotal
Employee Benefits
Tax

Total

As a child in Mexico, when I had a craving for something sweet, I would go out to the yard, pull a sweet potato from the ground or a papaya from the tree, and bring it to my mom to candy. She would boil it with syrup made from our cane sugar plants, but today I cook it with piloncillo, which tastes a lot like brown sugar, as well as some cinnamon and other spices. Eventually, a kind of caramel forms and coats the potato as it softens. Camote enmielado is a simple, albeit very sweet, snack or dessert that tastes delicious with a glass of milk.

CAMOTE ENMIELADO

Candied Sweet Potatoes ○ Serves 4 to 6

2 medium sweet potatoes, cleaned and cut into 2-inch-thick rounds

1 medium (8-ounce) cone piloncillo or ¾ cup brown sugar

3 star anise

1 large cinnamon stick, preferably Mexican

1 whole clove

1 teaspoon kosher salt

In a large pot, combine the sweet potatoes, 1 cup water, piloncillo, star anise, cinnamon, clove, and salt. Bring to a boil, then reduce to a simmer and let cook until the sweet potato is very soft and the liquid is thickened, about 1 hour. (If the liquid is still runny and not syrupy enough, remove the sweet potato and continue to cook the liquid at high heat until it reaches a syrupy texture.) Serve with syrup spooned over the sweet potato.

The best options for cooling off on a sunny day or hot night in Mexico, paletas are icy treats classically made from fresh tropical-fruit juices and purees—sort of like frozen agua fresca with a little extra sweetener. Growing up, when we didn't have fancy popsicle molds at home, we would freeze the fruit mixtures in little plastic bags, then snip a corner off to eat them. At Nopalito we've had some fun with our paletas, adding coffee, chocolate, and rice milk to the mix of flavors, as well as adding milk and cream to some of the fruit varieties for a richer taste.

PALETAS

Popsicles

Café con Leche

¾ cup coarsely ground coffee beans

2 medium (8-ounce) cones piloncillo or 1 cup brown sugar

2 cups heavy cream

Chocolate

¾ cinnamon stick, preferably Mexican

¾ cup unsweetened cocoa powder

1 cup sugar

6 ounces bittersweet chocolate (not chips), coarsely chopped or broken into pieces

CONTINUED

Paletas de Café con Leche

Coffee and Milk Popsicles ○ Makes 12

In a medium pot, combine the coffee, 2 cups water, and the piloncillo. Bring to a boil, stirring occasionally, then remove from the heat and let steep for 10 minutes, stirring occasionally to help the sugar dissolve.

Strain the mixture through a chinois or other very fine-mesh strainer into a bowl. Stir in the cream and let cool completely.

Pour into twelve 3-ounce paleta or popsicle molds, being sure to set the sticks while the mixture is still liquid. Freeze until firm, 6 to 8 hours. (If necessary to help extract the paletas, run the molds briefly under hot water.)

Paletas de Chocolate

Chocolate-Cinnamon Popsicles ○ Makes 12

In a small pot, combine 1 cup water and the cinnamon stick. Bring to a boil, then turn off the heat, cover the pot, and let steep while you make the popsicle base.

In a medium pot, whisk the cocoa powder and sugar into 3 cups water. Bring to a boil over medium heat, stirring to help dissolve the sugar, then immediately turn off the heat.

Place the bittersweet chocolate in a heatproof large bowl and pour the sugar-cocoa mixture over it. Add the cinnamon water and stir until the chocolate is fully melted.

Remove the cinnamon stick and pour the mixture into twelve 3-ounce paleta or popsicle molds, being sure to set the sticks while the mixture is still liquid. Freeze until firm, 6 to 8 hours. (If necessary to help extract the paletas, run the molds briefly under hot water.)

CONTINUED

Limón con Crema

1¼ cups heavy cream

¾ cup whole milk

¾ cup freshly squeezed
lime juice (from 6 limes)

¾ cup sugar

Zest of 1 lime

⅛ teaspoon kosher salt

Fresas

4 cups cleaned and
stemmed strawberries

¼ cup freshly squeezed
orange juice (from ½ orange)

½ cup agave nectar

Zest of ½ lime

⅛ teaspoon kosher salt

Mango con Chile

4 cups diced ripe mango,
plus ½ cup very finely
diced mango

¼ cup freshly squeezed
orange juice (from ½ orange)

½ cup agave nectar,
plus more as needed

⅛ teaspoon kosher salt

½ teaspoon Nopalito Spices
(page 35) or chile powder

Paletas de Limón con Crema

Lime Sherbet Popsicles ○ Makes 10

In a large bowl, combine the cream, milk, lime juice, ¾ cup water, sugar, lime zest, and salt and whisk until the sugar is dissolved.

Pour the mixture into ten 3-ounce paleta or popsicle molds, being sure to set the sticks while the mixture is still liquid. Freeze until firm, 6 to 8 hours. (If necessary to help extract the paletas, run the molds briefly under hot water.)

Paletas de Fresas

Strawberry Popsicles ○ Makes 10

In a blender, combine the strawberries, orange juice, agave nectar, ¼ cup water, lime zest, and salt; blend well until smooth.

Pour the mixture into ten 3-ounce paleta or popsicle molds, being sure to set the sticks while the mixture is still liquid. Freeze until firm, 6 to 8 hours. (If necessary to help extract the paletas, run the molds briefly under hot water.)

Paletas de Mango con Chile

Spicy Mango Popsicles ○ Makes 12

In a blender, combine the 4 cups diced mango, orange juice, agave nectar, and salt with ¼ cup water; blend until very smooth. Add the finely diced mango and Nopalito Spices and stir to combine. Taste and adjust the amount of agave as needed.

Pour the mixture into twelve 3-ounce paleta or popsicle molds, being sure to set the sticks while the mixture is still liquid. Freeze until firm, 6 to 8 hours. (If necessary to help extract the paletas, run the molds briefly under hot water.)

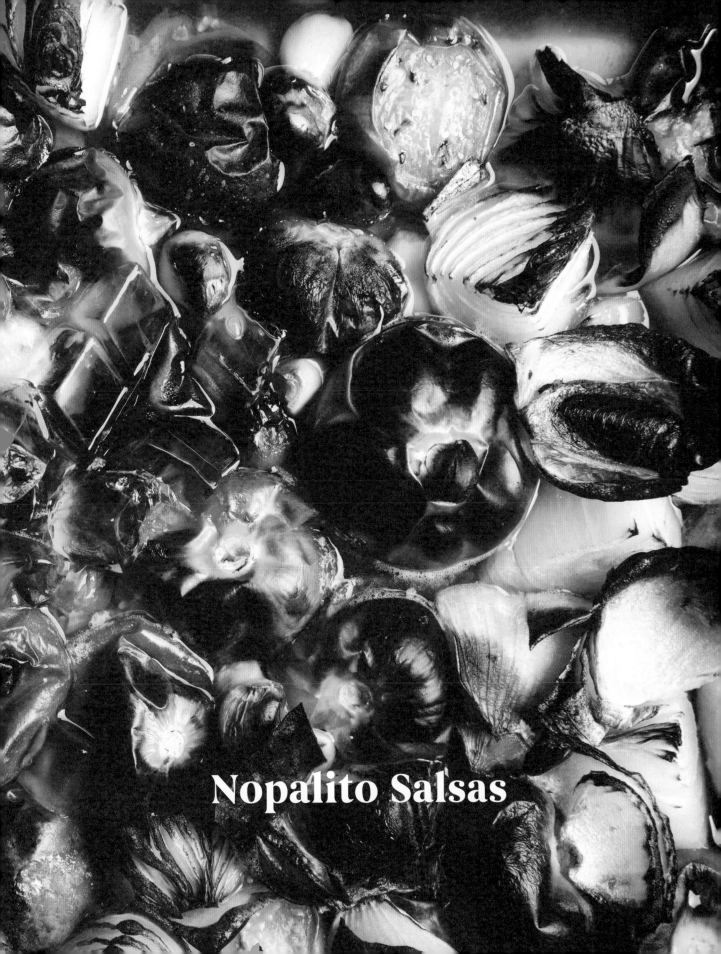

Nopalito Salsas

IF YOU WANT TO SEE A MEXICAN CHEF BEAM WITH PRIDE,

say something nice about the chef's salsa. As ubiquitous and expected as salsa may be in Mexican cooking, tasting one can tell you so much about a cook—perhaps where the cook grew up in Mexico; what kind of importance the cook places on quality ingredients, freshness, and seasonality; or even how much the cook knows about regional Mexican food.

Tasting a very special salsa, or one that is perfectly matched with a dish, can enliven the entire meal. Broadly categorized into red (*salsas rojas*) and green (*salsas verdes*), salsas have many uses in Mexican cooking far beyond being a dip for chips—in fact, that is something they're not really used for in Mexico. Most salsas are for topping antojitos, some are specifically for tacos (*salsas taqueras*), and still others are like what most people here in the States would call a hot sauce, commonly used for sprinkling on soups to add extra spice. Some salsas are used to marinate meats or fish or to act as the base of a braise or stew.

Your choice of salsa should be determined by how you intend to use it to bring balance to a dish. Some are sweet, others tangy and acidic; some are smoky or have a charred flavor from grilled ingredients, while others are extremely spicy; and many have different textures and flavors based on whether the ingredients are raw or cooked, served chunky, or pureed until smooth.

The trick to top-notch flavor in salsas is to learn about the building blocks and basic techniques—sampling how different chiles taste when toasted to certain degrees, seeing what happens when you hold down the blender button for just a few seconds more, and experimenting with ingredients both raw and cooked to notice their flavor differences. All of these little factors contribute to a salsa's final flavor, color, and consistency, and can provide the kick of heat or coolness your taste buds need.

Our salsas at Nopalito are largely based on traditional flavors from various regions of Mexico. But at times I have tweaked and improvised them a little, based on wanting a perfect flavor to suit a certain dish, with a small shift in texture, heat level, smokiness, or acidity. Some are intended to use with a specific dish; others are all-purpose. While there are probably even more types of salsa in the world than there are cooks who make them, the endless combinations should motivate and amaze us as cooks, rather than intimidate us. Hey, it's just a salsa. How hard can it be? If nothing else, remember this: just five or ten minutes of kitchen assembly pays off in a homemade salsa that you can draw on in your refrigerator for up to one week.

This is a very special salsa—complex, nutty, and rich, yet vinegary, with a nice moderate-to-strong level of heat. We use sunflower seeds in our recipe, but salsa macha is traditionally made with coarsely ground peanuts. You can really taste the dried oregano, which gives it an herbaceous quality, and the sunflower seeds, which give it a bit of body and even a slightly grainy texture, making this a great option for dunking chips or quesadillas into.

Keep a close eye on the chiles while they are roasting. They can burn quickly, which will give the salsa a bitter taste and dark color.

SALSA MACHA

Makes about ¾ cup

¼ cup raw unsalted sunflower seeds

12 medium dried chiles de árbol, stemmed and seeded

1 dried ancho chile, stemmed and seeded

2 tablespoons white vinegar

2 medium cloves garlic

1½ teaspoons dried oregano

¼ cup olive oil

Salt

Preheat the oven to 350°F. Add the sunflower seeds and chiles to a small baking sheet. Roast for 2 minutes, then remove the chiles (leave the sunflower seeds on the pan); continue to roast the seeds until lightly toasted, about 5 minutes more.

Transfer the chiles to a medium heatproof bowl and add boiling water to cover; let soak until softened, about 20 minutes.

Transfer the chiles (reserve the soaking water) to a blender; puree until a thick paste forms, adding a little of the soaking water only as needed to help blend. Add the toasted sunflower seeds, vinegar, garlic, and oregano; with the motor running, slowly drizzle in the oil until the salsa is emulsified but still lightly chunky. Taste and adjust the seasoning as necessary.

This is an all-purpose salsa verde to serve with chips, tacos, enchiladas, or savory breakfasts. Boiling the tomatillos and chiles not only helps to sweeten and mellow the flavor of the tomatillos but also gives this salsa a creamier texture and subtler green color. Be sure to taste the jalapeños before you get started to see how spicy they are, since their heat level can vary greatly, changing the heat level of the salsa as well.

SALSA CILANTRO

Makes about 2 cups

8 large tomatillos (about 1 pound), husked and rinsed

1 to 2 jalapeños

2 cloves garlic

Salt

2 tablespoons chopped cilantro leaves

2 tablespoons chopped white onion

In a medium pot, combine the tomatillos, jalapeños, and garlic; add enough water just to cover and season with salt. Bring to a boil, then reduce to a simmer and let cook for 15 minutes, or until the tomatillos and jalapeños begin to dull in color.

Transfer the tomatillos, jalapeños, and garlic (discard the water) to a blender and blend until the salsa is somewhat smooth but you can still see the seeds of the tomatillos.

Pour the salsa into a bowl and refrigerate until chilled. Stir in the cilantro and onions just before serving. Taste and adjust the seasoning if necessary.

This is a very spicy salsa, but its appeal is more than just its heat—it also has a fruity flavor and interesting texture, more like a chunky, fresh pico de gallo than a pureed salsa. You can add or subtract the number of habaneros to adjust the spice level if desired, but thanks to all the fresh citrus juice, the heat level is not unbearable.

To keep the spice off your fingertips, use gloves while working with the habaneros.

HABANERO SALSA

Makes about 2 cups

1 small white onion, finely chopped

1 cup freshly squeezed lime juice (from about 6 limes)

1 cup freshly squeezed orange juice (from 3 to 4 oranges)

3 to 4 small habanero chiles, finely diced

Leaves from ½ bunch cilantro, chopped

Salt

In a medium bowl, combine the onions and lime juice; let sit at least 5 minutes, allowing the onions to start pickling. Stir in the orange juice, habaneros, cilantro, and a pinch of salt. Add more salt as needed to taste.

Moritas are among the spiciest of the dark dried chiles, but this salsa is still only slightly-to-moderately spicy. The chiles have more of a well-rounded smoky flavor, and a fruity, jammy quality when reconstituted. I like to leave this salsa relatively chunky, so you can still see the seeds and some of the texture of the aromatics. It is excellent atop tacos, but you can really use it for anything.

SALSA DE MORITA CON TOMATILLO

Makes about 2 cups

12 medium tomatillos, husked and rinsed

1 tablespoon rice bran oil or canola oil

6 medium dried morita chiles, stemmed

3 cloves garlic

½ white onion

Salt

Preheat the oven to 400°F. Place the tomatillos on a medium ovenproof skillet or small rimmed baking sheet. Roast until the tomatillos are slightly browned and look charred on top, about 20 minutes. Remove and let cool.

In a small pot, heat the oil over medium-high heat. Add the chiles and cook, turning frequently, until blistered in places but not burned, 30 to 40 seconds. Pour enough water into the pan to cover the chiles, then bring the water to a simmer. Let simmer until the chiles are very soft, about 25 minutes. Remove the chiles and discard the soaking water.

In a molcajete or a food processor, process the chiles into a paste. Add the garlic and onions and continue to process until the mixture is finely ground. Remove the mixture to a medium serving bowl and add the tomatillos to the molcajete or food processor. Process until jammy (you will still be able to see the seeds and some chunkiness). Stir the tomatillos into the bowl and season with salt to taste.

Unlike the usual table salsa, salsa de morita is more like a paste to be used as a spread for cemitas and other sandwiches. The combination of dark, medium-heat chiles and piloncillo gives this salsa a flavor reminiscent of a spicy-sweet barbecue sauce.

This is one of the rare examples of a salsa that must be cooked for a while. Because of this, the flavors and spiciness tend to concentrate, so you may want to start with fewer chiles if you are sensitive to heat.

2 cups stemmed dried morita chiles

¼ cup white vinegar

1 tablespoon ground piloncillo or brown sugar

¼ white onion, coarsely chopped

2 whole cloves

1 bay leaf

1 clove garlic

1½ teaspoons kosher salt, plus more as needed

¾ teaspoon dried oregano

¾ teaspoon dried thyme

¼ teaspoon ground cinnamon

1 cup olive oil

SALSA DE MORITA

Makes about 4 cups

In a small pot, combine all of the ingredients except the oil with 4 cups water. Bring to a boil, then reduce to a simmer; cover the pot and let cook at a low simmer, stirring occasionally, for 2 hours.

Transfer the mixture to a blender and puree until very smooth. With the blender motor running, slowly add the olive oil, blending until incorporated. Taste and add more salt as needed.

Chile de árbol is one of my favorite chiles to use; it is addictively spicy. When you pan-fry these slender red chiles, they take on a really unique toasted quality. I love this salsa on everything, but especially with rich dishes or fried foods like meaty empanadas.

In the summer, you can substitute fresh tomatoes (I prefer the Early Girl variety) for the canned version. You may have to add a little extra water to thin the consistency.

2 tablespoons rice bran oil or canola oil

2 dried árbol chiles, stemmed and seeded

1 clove garlic, chopped

2 cups canned diced tomatoes and their juices

Salt

SALSA FRITA DE ÁRBOL

Makes about 3 cups

In a small skillet, heat the oil over medium heat. Add the chiles and cook, turning occasionally, until they are bright red and aromatic, 15 to 20 seconds. Transfer the chiles to a plate and set aside. In the same oil, sauté the garlic, stirring constantly, until lightly golden-brown, about 1 minute. Add the tomatoes and a generous pinch of salt and bring to a boil, then reduce to a simmer and let cook for 10 minutes.

Transfer the mixture to a blender and puree until very smooth. Add water as needed to adjust the consistency. Taste and adjust the salt. Serve warm or cool.

Unlike a cooked tomatillo salsa, this version retains all the bracing freshness and acidity of its raw ingredients. It has a crisp, rustic texture, so much so that you can still see tiny pieces of the skins after it's been blitzed in the food processor. The heat of the raw jalapeños also shines right through.

Because of these qualities, salsa cruda tastes best drizzled atop some kind of meat-based antojitos or entrées (such as carnitas), or at least a dish with very robust, "meaty" vegetables, like grilled portobello or king oyster mushrooms. It is a little too raw-tasting to eat on its own with chips.

1 to 2 jalapeños, coarsely chopped

7 medium tomatillos, husked and rinsed

1 large clove garlic

Leaves from ¼ bunch cilantro

Salt

SALSA CRUDA

Makes 2 cups

In a food processor, combine the jalapeños, tomatillos, garlic, cilantro, and a generous pinch of salt; pulse until the ingredients are well blended but the salsa still has a slightly chunky texture. Taste and adjust the amount of chiles and salt as desired.

SALSA DE SERRANO
Y TOMATILLO

SALSA CHILTOMATE

SALSA ESCABECHE

PEQUIN
HOT SAUCE

SALSA DE
MORITA

SALSA CILANTRO

SALSA BORRACHA

HABANERO SALSA

SALSA CRUDA

Because of this salsa's red-orange color, saucy quality, and sweetness, in a blind tasting you might guess that it contains tomatoes. In reality, the flavor and color all come from the chiles. The mild, brightly colored guajillo and spicier árbol chiles are blended with a fair amount of oil, which emulsifies to give the salsa a smooth, creamy texture. It pairs well with fried empanadas, and I like it spooned over tacos as well.

To get this salsa as smooth as possible (especially if you don't have a high-powered blender), you can strain it to remove any stubborn pieces of chile skin that remain. Or, to turn it into a chunkier salsa—better for dipping chips into—you can stir in some finely chopped white onion and cilantro at the end.

SALSA FRITA DE GUAJILLO

Makes 2 cups

¼ cup rice bran oil or canola oil, for frying

4 medium dried guajillo chiles, stemmed and seeded

¼ cup dried árbol chiles, stemmed and seeded

2 cloves garlic

2 medium tomatillos, husked and rinsed

½ medium white onion, coarsely chopped

Salt

In a small pot over medium heat, heat the oil until very hot (about 350°F). Add the chiles and cook, turning frequently with tongs or a spoon, until dark red, about 10 seconds. Remove the chiles immediately.

Transfer to a heatproof bowl and add enough boiling water to cover; let soak until the chiles are softened, about 20 minutes.

Transfer the chiles to a blender (discard the soaking water). Add the garlic, tomatillos, and onion and a generous pinch of salt and puree until smooth.

Pour the salsa into a medium pot and bring to a boil; reduce to a simmer and let cook for about 10 minutes. Taste and adjust the seasoning as needed. Use warm or cool.

This three-ingredient salsa verde is traditionally served alongside empanadas in the north of Mexico. Its raw-tasting, tangy sourness and kick of heat are meant to help cut through some of the fattiness of fried masa pastries, so it is best used on similarly rich, fatty foods (it's not so great on its own with chips).

If you happen to get a mild jalapeño, feel free to increase the amount of chile to achieve more heat.

4 large tomatillos, husked and rinsed

1 to 2 jalapeños, or more to taste

2 teaspoons freshly squeezed lime juice

Salt

SALSA DE TOMATILLO Y JALAPEÑO

Makes about 1½ cups

In a blender, combine the tomatillos, jalapeño, and lime juice; blend until the mixture is somewhat chunky and you can still see the seeds of the tomatillos. Season with salt to taste.

With a clean, vinegary acidity thanks to the inclusion of pickled jalapeños and vegetables, this extra-chunky salsa goes well with almost anything—from delicate seafood to fatty, hearty comfort foods. It makes a great condiment on a meaty sandwich and brightens up the flavor of braised or refried beans.

SALSA ESCABECHE

Makes about 3 cups

2 cups Jalapeños Curtidos (page 39) or jarred mixed pickled vegetables, coarsely chopped

1 cup (8 ounces) canned diced tomatoes and their juices

Salt

In a food processor, combine the pickles and tomatoes; pulse until chunky. Taste and add salt if needed.

The word for "drunk" in Mexico is *borracho* (*borracha* in the feminine form)—which is how this beer-and-tequila-containing salsa earns its name. Lamb is my favorite meat to serve with it, but its dried-fruit flavor and rich texture also make it a good match with beef dishes such as carne asada. The addition of apple juice, sugar, and tomatillos delivers some sweetness and tartness to counteract its little kick of heat and smokiness. But it is on the milder side.

SALSA BORRACHA

Makes about 3 cups

5 dried pasilla chiles, stemmed and seeded

1 dried mulato chile, stemmed and seeded

3 medium tomatillos, husked and rinsed

2 cloves garlic

2 tablespoons ground piloncillo or brown sugar

½ cup apple juice

Salt

1 small white onion, finely diced

½ cup dark Mexican beer, such as Negra Modelo

2 tablespoons good-quality tequila (optional)

Preheat a griddle or skillet over high heat. Add all of the chiles and let cook, turning every 10 seconds or so, until they start to blister and darken but do not burn, about 1 minute. Transfer to a heatproof bowl and cover with boiling water; let sit until softened, about 20 minutes.

Meanwhile, preheat the same griddle again over high heat. Add the tomatillos and garlic and cook, turning occasionally, until charred, about 10 minutes.

Transfer the softened chiles to a blender (reserve the soaking water). Add one tomatillo to the blender and pulse until the mixture is chunky. Add the remaining tomatillos and the garlic, piloncillo, apple juice, and a pinch of salt, and blend until chunky. Transfer to a bowl and add the onions, beer, and tequila. Taste and adjust the seasoning, or thin with the reserved soaking water, as needed.

As the name implies, this chunky, simple, but very spicy salsa features chiles and tomatoes as its two main ingredients. It comes from the Yucatán region in the south of Mexico, where some local versions of this salsa are as simple as these two ingredients charred, pureed together, and seasoned with salt. In this case I added some toasted onions and garlic for a little more complexity. You can stir in some chopped cilantro leaves at the end for color.

I like salsa chiltomate best with heartier dishes that can stand up to its habanero-derived heat and benefit from the acidity of the tomatoes. Although, if you are okay with the heat, you can eat this salsa straight with chips, too.

SALSA CHILTOMATE

Makes about 2½ cups

2 cups canned diced tomatoes and their juices

¼ white onion

1 small clove garlic

1 habanero chile, any color, stemmed and halved

Salt

Chopped fresh cilantro leaves (optional)

Preheat the oven to 450°F. Place the tomatoes in a roasting pan and pour in ½ cup water. Roast until the tops of the tomatoes are darkened and charred, 20 to 30 minutes. Remove and let cool (reserve the liquid).

Meanwhile, heat a griddle or large skillet to medium-high heat and add the onion, garlic, and habanero. Cook, rotating the vegetables every few minutes until they are completely charred on the outside, about 20 minutes. Remove and let cool slightly.

Transfer the onion, garlic, and half of the habanero (discard the stem but reserve the other half) to a molcajete or a food processor. Process until chunky, then add the tomatoes, working in batches if necessary, and continue to process until broken down significantly but still a little chunky. Pour into a bowl, season with salt, add the cilantro if using, and stir well, adding some of the pan liquid if needed for consistency. Taste and add more salt and/or the remaining half of the chile (finely grind it first) to taste if desired.

When making this salsa, the charring step is the most important. You want to cook the vegetables at a scorching-hot temperature so that their skins blacken while their interiors remain somewhat untouched (you can also do this step over a high-heat wood or charcoal fire). The end product is a salsa that retains some of its biting freshness while taking on fire-cooked flavor. It is delicious on scrambled or poached eggs in the morning, but you can use it on anything and everything.

Because serrano chiles can sometimes be very spicy, start with a little; you can add more as desired.

SALSA DE SERRANO Y TOMATILLO

Makes 4 cups

10 medium tomatillos, husked, rinsed, and patted dry

1 to 4 serrano chiles

½ white onion, plus ¼ cup finely chopped white onion

2 cloves garlic

Salt

¼ cup chopped fresh cilantro leaves

Preheat the oven to 450°F. Place the tomatillos, 1 or more of the chiles, the ½ onion, and the garlic in a roasting pan. Roast, flipping the tomatillos and chiles halfway through, until the skins are blackened all over, about 20 minutes. Remove and let cool slightly.

Using a molcajete or a food processor, process the roasted ingredients to a slightly chunky consistency. Transfer to a medium serving bowl, season generously with salt, and stir well. Taste and adjust the roasted chile and salt amounts as needed. Stir in the chopped onion and cilantro.

Inspired by a beloved bottled hot sauce in Mexico, this salsa has a smooth consistency and good amount of vinegar, but it's not super spicy.

SALSA "BUFALO"

Makes about 1 cup

3 dried guajillo chiles, stemmed and seeded

1 dried árbol chile, stemmed and seeded

¾ cup white vinegar

Salt

In a blender, combine all of the chiles, vinegar, a pinch of salt, and 2 tablespoons water; blend until very smooth. Strain through a fine-mesh strainer.

Salsa de árbol is a smooth, saucy salsa that is high in acid and tartness thanks to the tomatoes, tomatillos, and vinegar. You can use this salsa as the base for chilaquiles, tossed onto chips or totopos (page 64), or spooned atop any antojito or entrée that contains a lot of fat, like a braised meat or stew such as Birria al Res (page 151). The salsa's acidity will help add contrast and cut the richness of these dishes.

This salsa is not quite as spicy as the Salsa Frita de Árbol (page 222), but it is still quite impressively spicy.

SALSA DE ÁRBOL

Makes about 2 cups

1 tablespoon olive oil

Scant ¼ cup dried árbol chiles, stemmed and seeded

1½ cups (12 ounces) canned diced tomatoes and their juices

1 small tomatillo

2 tablespoons white vinegar

1 small clove garlic

½ teaspoon kosher salt, plus more as needed

In a small pot, heat the oil over high heat, then add the chiles; let cook, continuously tossing the chiles so that they do not burn, about 10 seconds. When they turn bright orange, they are done. Immediately remove from the oil.

Add three-quarters of the chiles to a blender and reserve the rest. Add the tomatoes, tomatillo, vinegar, garlic, salt, and 2 tablespoons water and blend until smooth. Taste and adjust the seasoning, or blend in more of the remaining chiles, to taste.

Pour the blended salsa into a small pot, bring to a boil, then reduce the heat and let simmer for 15 minutes. Serve warm or cool.

This smooth, fruity, mild red salsa has a very particular use: I dunk tortillas (see Tortas Pambazos, page 160) or torta rolls (see Enchiladas Rojas de Camarón, page 167) into it until they are completely coated, then sear them on a hot griddle. The salsa caramelizes and sets, turning the tortillas and rolls an alluring shade of red and giving them a vibrant chile flavor.

Since the salsa contains some raw ingredients that taste better once they are pan-fried, I'd stick to recommended uses—you really don't want to eat this salsa raw.

SALSA GUAJILLO

Makes about 1 cup

2 dried mulato chiles, stemmed and seeded

3 dried guajillo chiles, stemmed and seeded

2 cloves garlic

¼ white onion, diced

¾ cup (6 ounces) canned diced tomatoes and their juices

½ teaspoon dried oregano

½ teaspoon ground cumin

Salt

Place all of the chiles in a medium heatproof bowl and cover with boiling water; let sit until softened, about 20 minutes.

Transfer the chiles (reserve the soaking water) to a blender. Add the garlic, onion, tomatoes, oregano, cumin, and a pinch of salt and puree until very smooth, adding some of the soaking water only if needed to blend. Taste and adjust the seasoning as necessary.

This is one of the spiciest things we offer in the restaurant. It's a homemade pequin chile–based version of the Mexican-style hot sauces you commonly see in stores or restaurants—vinegary and a little smoky, with a little tomato for balance. Because of the vinegar, it can keep in the fridge for weeks or even months. It's a great all-purpose hot sauce, and I love it on soups, pozoles, birrias, or anything else.

PEQUIN HOT SAUCE

Makes 2 cups

¼ cup dried pequin chiles, stemmed

¼ cup dried árbol chiles, stemmed

1 tablespoon plus 1 teaspoon tomato paste

1 large clove garlic

2 tablespoons chopped white onion

1¼ cups distilled white vinegar

1 cup olive oil (not extra-virgin), or half olive oil and half rice bran oil

In a blender, combine all of the ingredients along with ¼ cup water; blend until very smooth. Strain through a fine-mesh strainer. Store in an airtight container in the refrigerator for up to several weeks.

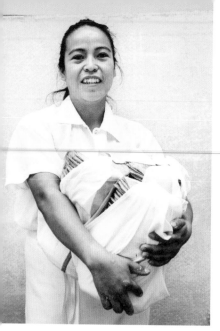

GRACIAS

Making this book was such an amazing adventure. I would like to thank all of the people who work so hard in our restaurants every day behind the scenes, making Nopalito the special place it is without asking for even an ounce of credit. I want to thank my partners, especially Laurence Jossel, my chef partner, whom I was so lucky to meet when I first arrived in San Francisco, and who gave me the opportunity to do what I now love doing most. Thank you for believing in me and giving me many opportunities, but most of all the chance to cook the food on which I was raised. You have always pushed me to do things that I didn't think I could do, and this book is just one example. I also want to sincerely thank our other partners, Jeff and Ally, for being a huge part of my work life as well as my life outside work. You three are now a part of my family.

I am grateful for all of the people who have made Nopalito possible—who were a part of it for even just a day, and of course those who have been with us since day one: Lidia Guzman, Sergio Guzman, Benjamin Guzman, Jose Guadalupe, Luis Chan, Gabino Aguilar, Irma Bacab, Christian Maldonado, and my former co-chef, Jose Ramos. I am sure I have forgotten some names, but you know who you are.

I also want to thank my friend and coauthor, Stacy Adimando, for writing so beautifully, and for taking this cookbook journey with me. Also, the good people at Ten Speed Press and photographer Eva Kolenko—I owe it to you for making this book so beautiful.

Thanks sincerely to all of the hard-working recipe testers who went above and beyond to make sure the recipes were the best they could be. We are indebted to you.

Finally, I really want to thank my family, who have always been there for me in every moment, even the times I was working too many hours and couldn't be with them at home. I love you, and you mean everything to me. And to my family in Mexico, especially my mom—I had to leave her at such a young age, and she has always said she wished she could have given me more or sent me to college. Mom, I want to tell you just one more time: I did get all that I needed, and so much more.

Thank you, everyone, from the bottom of my heart, for making this possible.

—*Gonzalo*

INDEX

Copyright © 2017 by Gonzalo Guzmán
Photographs copyright © 2017 by Eva Kolenko

Published in the United States by Ten Speed Press, an imprint
of the Crown Publishing Group, a division of Penguin Random
House LLC, New York.
www.crownpublishing.com
www.tenspeed.com

Ten Speed Press and the Ten Speed Press colophon are
registered trademarks of Penguin Random House LLC.

Library of Congress Cataloging-in-Publication Data

Names:Guzmán, Gonzalo González, author. | Adimando, Stacy.
    | Kolenko, Eva, photographer (expression)
Title: Nopalito : a Mexican kitchen / Gonzalo González Guzmán,
    with Stacy Adimando ; photography by Eva Kolenko.
Description: First edition. | Berkeley : Ten Speed Press, 2017.
    | Includes bibliographical references and index.
Identifiers: LCCN 2016030890 (print) | LCCN 2016040850
    (ebook) | ISBN 9780399578281 (hardback) | ISBN
    9780399578298 (Ebook)
Subjects: LCSH: Cooking, Mexican. | Nopalito (Restaurant) |
    BISAC: COOKING / Regional & Ethnic / Mexican. | COOKING
    / Regional & Ethnic / American / California Style. | LCGFT:
    Cookbooks.
Classification: LCC TX716.M4 G897 2017 (print) | LCC TX716.M4
    (ebook) | DDC 641.5972—dc23
LC record available at https://lccn.loc.gov/2016030890

Printed in China

Design by Emma Campion and Margaux Keres
Prop Stylist Clair Mack

10 9 8 7 6 5 4 3 2 1

First Edition